Village Walks
— in —
NORTHAMPTONSHIRE

C000111180

Judy Smith

COUNTRYSIDE BOOKS
NEWBURY, BERKSHIRE

First published 1999
© Judy Smith 1999

All rights reserved.
No reproduction permitted without the prior
permission of the publisher:

COUNTRYSIDE BOOKS
3 Catherine Road
Newbury, Berkshire

ISBN 1 85306 561 7

Designed by Graham Whiteman
Photographs by Reginald Hayes
Maps by the author
Illustrations by Trevor Yorke

Front cover showing footpath to King's Sutton,
supplied by Bill Meadows.

Produced through MRM Associates Ltd., Reading
Printed by J. W. Arrowsmith Ltd., Bristol

Contents

Area Map Showing Locations of the Walks.

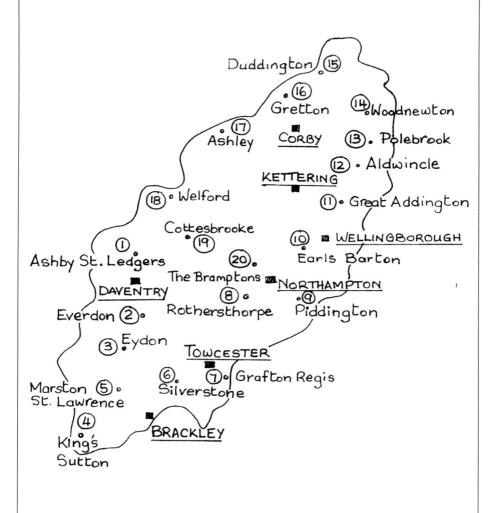

WALK

Publisher's Note

We hope that you obtain considerable enjoyment from this book; great care has been taken in its preparation. Although at the time of publication all routes followed public rights of way or permitted paths, diversion orders can be made and permissions withdrawn.

We cannot of course be held responsible for such diversion orders and any inaccuracies in the text which result from these or any other changes to the routes nor any damage which might result from walkers trespassing on private property. We are anxious though that all details covering the walks are kept up to date and would therefore welcome information from readers which would be relevant to future editions.

Introduction

It is well worth taking time to discover the secrets of the villages of Northamptonshire. And in doing so you will be something of a pioneer – even now one of the few to explore this 'forgotten' county. Northamptonshire is for many just a place to hurry through. Most of the great transport routes north from London are here – the M1, the railway, and even the Grand Union Canal. Perhaps it is less forgotten than unknown!

There is no doubt that its villages are one of Northamptonshire's greatest assets. The charm of these villages lies in part in the subtle colours of the stone used for building. Northamptonshire lies on the great Jurassic ridge, the limestone belt that runs from Dorset to the Humber. Many of the villages are of silver grey limestone, sometimes impregnated with iron ore, giving the stone a warm brown appearance. The stones are often mixed, as in the churches at Gretton and Ashley. Near Northampton, villages may be of deep brown or orange sandstone, a surprisingly intense colour, as at Eydon and The Bramptons. And historically these are ancient villages, old even before the Domesday Book was compiled.

Every village has its church, and many have a manor house, too. Not for nothing has Northamptonshire been dubbed the county of 'Spires and Squires'. The churches of Northamptonshire are amongst the finest in England, and here you will have the opportunity of visiting some that are quite unique. At Earls Barton there is a fine Saxon tower, over 1,000 years old, at Ashley the interior was restored by Gilbert Scott, while at Ashby st Ledgers, the wall paintings are justly famous. The walks pass some of Northamptonshire's many manor houses and stately homes, and you can contrast the complexity and sheer size of Kirby Hall with the tranquil setting of Cottesbrooke Hall or the Norman grandeur of Rockingham Castle. History is in these villages, too. You can visit Bronze Age tumuli, a Roman villa site, a Saxon battleground, deserted medieval villages, the house where the Gunpowder Plot was hatched or the site of the Civil War Battle of Naseby.

Walking is surprisingly good in Northamptonshire. Seven long-distance paths pass through the county and the footpaths are well maintained through each parish by a volunteer Parish Path Warden. You should find the routes to be well-marked and clear of obstruction. In each walk you have been provided with a sketch map, but you may also find the appropriate Ordnance Survey Landranger map to be of help. I should sound one note of caution! Although normally quite obvious, at ploughing time some of the cross-field paths may be temporarily obliterated. Where possible I have tried to point out landmarks which will help you to find your way.

Northamptonshire is entirely an agricultural county. As the 17th-century Northamptonshire historian, Thomas Fuller put it, 'there is little waste ground' – meaning there are no wild places! Nevertheless, these walks will give you some wonderful views. You can look out along the Welland Valley from the limestone ridge at Ashley, or take in the scene from the top of Haselbech Hill. Above Great Addington, there is a viewpoint from which twelve churches in the Nene Valley can be seen. You will also cross parkland, as at Eydon and Fawsley, and wander beside river and canal. At Aldwincle, you walk through a nature reserve, and at Duddington, through the great Rockingham Forest.

The villages in this book are a selection of my favourites. Each village is here for its beauty, its history or purely its character – and some exhibit all three. The walks, too, are not all the best-known, but still some of the finest in Northamptonshire. And I have no doubt that this county should be famous for its pubs also – testing the entries in this book has been purest pleasure! There are also suggested Places of Interest nearby, to help make your day especially enjoyable.

And now, in conclusion, I would like to thank those who helped with this book. Firstly, I am indebted to my husband Eric, my daughter Amy and those many friends, especially Geoff and Ros Crook, who tried the walks and painstakingly checked the directions. I am also grateful to my father, Reginald Hayes, who took all the photographs.

I wish you well in your journey through Northamptonshire. The entries in this book have been arranged in an order that will allow you, should you wish, to devise your own walk from one village to the next on footpaths, using an Ordnance Survey map. The round distance would be some 200 miles, a wonderful tour of Northamptonshire. I wonder if anyone will take up the challenge? Good luck!

Judy Smith

ASHBY ST LEDGERS

Length: 5 miles

Getting there: Ashby St Ledgers lies just east of the A361, 4 miles north of Daventry.	**Parking:** On quiet roadsides in the village.	**Map:** OS Landranger 152 Northampton and Milton Keynes (GR 573682).

The year was 1605. Queen Elizabeth had been dead for two years, and the new King James, despite his promises of clemency, was persecuting the Catholics even more vigorously than his predecessor. At the Manor House in Ashby St Ledgers lived one Robert Catesby, a young Catholic gentleman of great personality, bold, dashing, and a natural leader. Here, in the gatehouse to the manor, he gathered together a group of like-minded colleagues, and here they planned the most famous act of treason in British history – the Gunpowder Plot.

Four hundred years on, the gatehouse and manor are well-preserved. You can stand in this attractive village street and imagine the candlelit clandestine meetings, and the terror of their final reunion after their gallop from London the

FOOD and DRINK

The first inn you pass is the Stag's Head, beside the canal at Watford Gap. In winter there is a warm welcome at the unusual bar (boat-shaped) with open fireplace. On a summer's day, it is pure pleasure to sit on the sunny terraces overlooking the canal. The food here is excellent. The restaurant is 'award-winning' and the bar snacks menu reflects this quality too. Telephone: 01327 703621. The White Horse Inn at Welton is a genuine village pub with a friendly atmosphere, which serves – attractively – a comprehensive bill of fare seven days a week. The 'Ploughman's' is definitely to be recommended! Telephone: 01327 702820. When you return to Ashby St Ledgers, you can enjoy The Olde Coach Inn – and 'Olde' it is, all nooks and crannies, wooden benches and beams. The impressive menu is a gourmet's delight. It is a free house – and on a fine day you can repair to the attractive garden (with play area) to enjoy your repast. This is justly a very popular pub. Telephone: 01788 890349.

night the treachery was discovered at the Houses of Parliament. Robert Catesby was shot dead three days later at Holbeach Hall in Staffordshire, and his fellow conspirators were captured and later executed in the Tower. Catesby's elderly mother was allowed to live on at the manor until her death six years later. Some said she had master-minded the whole affair!

The Manor House you see today was enlarged and remodelled by Sir Edwin Lutyens at the beginning of the 20th century. The additions are obvious. There is also a strange half-timbered wing which is actually an Elizabethan house from Ipswich relocated here! More of Lutyens' work can be seen at the opposite end of the village – the fine row of thatched cottages opposite the Coach Inn.

Beside the manor is the church, dedi-

cated to St Mary the Virgin and that saint with the unpronounceable name, St Leodegarius. No wonder that it was corrupted to Ledgers! The church is quite remarkable, and, happily, is usually open to visitors. The pews are the originals from the 14th century and there are numerous fine brasses. But the medieval wall paintings are magnificent, perhaps the best Passion series in this country.

When you can tear yourself away from all this, a fine walk awaits you. The route follows the Jurassic Way signs from Ashby to the Grand Union Canal near Watford. Here, the A5, railway, M1 and canal all run side by side through Watford Gap, the natural Midland watershed. We choose – wisely! – to follow the canal, and this you can enjoy for some 2 miles before turning across fields to the pretty village of Welton. Another well-marked field path returns you to Ashby St Ledgers.

THE WALK

❶ Follow the Jurassic Way signs down a lane beside the church. At the field, bear right away from the Manor grounds to a stile at the top of the hill. Follow the obvious path through the copse ahead and then diagonally across the next field to a stile in the opposite fence. The path then runs along beside a small stream to reach the railway line.

❷ Cross the lines carefully where indicated! Then follow the stream again to come to the A5 road. Once across this, follow the Jurassic Way signs up the narrow path to Watford Locks and cross over the canal.

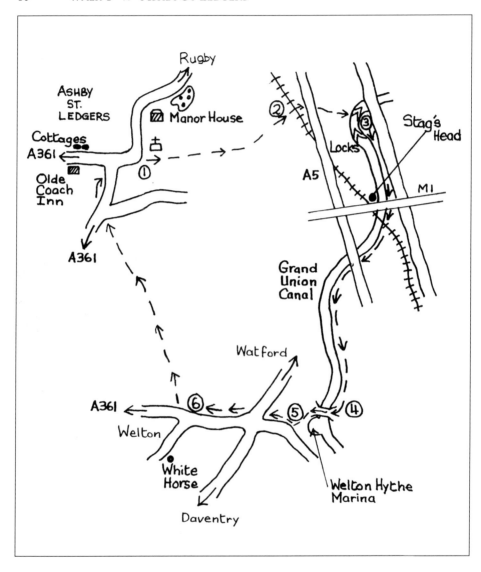

❸ Here you leave the Jurassic Way and turn right down the canal towpath. This is the Leicester Arm of the Grand Union Canal and you can enjoy the watery scene for nearly 2 miles until you come to the bridge immediately before Welton Hythe Marina.

❹ Leave the canal here, cross over the bridge, and follow the track around behind the marina buildings. When you reach the field, turn right away from the marina and, keeping the hedge on your right, walk gently uphill on what is, in fact, a bridleway.

The Manor House, Ashby St Ledgers.

❺ Eventually, pass through a gate on to a narrow road and keep straight ahead. At the crossroads, go straight over and in a further ¼ mile you will reach the village of Welton.

❻ At the road junction, keep to the right. (The road to the left descends into the main part of the village, which is most attractive. The White Horse Inn is about 100 yards from the junction.) Continuing along Ashby Road, in about 200 yards you will come to a footpath sign on the right. Following this will lead you out on to a field path, the direction of which should be marked by metal poles with white discs.

These poles will lead you through the fields all the way to Ashby. The path emerges at a road junction, and you follow the direction on the signpost to return to the village.

PLACES of INTEREST

Daventry Country Park is 4 miles south, on the outskirts of Daventry. Here, in summer, you can make up to the children for the lack of ice-cream on the walk! You can also offer them a most exciting adventure playground. If you should feel like more exercise, there are walks around the reservoir and meadow and you can visit bird-watching hides overlooking the water.

EVERDON

Length: 7 miles

Getting there: Everdon lies 2 miles south of the A45 Northampton-Daventry Road. Turn where signposted 1 mile west of Weedon Bec.	Parking: Quiet roadsides, especially near the church.	Map: OS Landranger 152 Northampton and Milton Keynes (GR 595574).

After the Battle of Hastings, William the Conqueror was feeling grateful to his half-brother, the Bishop of Bayeux, whose prayers on the field of battle he felt had undoubtedly influenced the outcome! He offered him many lands in England, but the Bishop is reputed to have asked specially for the Manor of Everdon, saying it was the most beautiful place he had seen on all his travels. Nearly 1,000 years later, you may well feel inclined to agree with him!

For many years the Bishop of Bayeux remained Lord of the Manor, although he ruled from distant France. He invited the Benedictine monks of Bernay in Normandy to set up a monastery here,

FOOD and DRINK

The Plough Inn at Everdon is a welcoming village pub with a menu which could not be wider. In addition to all the usual fare, there are always 'monthly specials' – about a dozen of them at a time! From this list you may choose lamb, red wine and plums or pork, orange and wild mushrooms, while the vegetarian choices are 'different' – try cashewnut paella! Excellent value, too. Telephone: 01327 361606.

which they did on the site of the present manor house. They later built the church, too, bringing in a family of French stonemasons called the de Corvilles to do the job. The de Corvilles also liked Everdon and stayed – their descendants (the name now corrupted to Carvell) still live in the area today.

A walk through the village will give you a glimpse of life here in earlier times – the names of the houses tell the tale! In the heart of Everdon, St Mary's church stands proudly looking out over the valley, a beautiful old building of warm brown stone. In the mid 1700s, the vicar here was one William Antrobus. He was the uncle of scholar and poet Thomas Gray, perhaps most famous for his *Elegy written in a Country Churchyard*. Thomas Gray visited his uncle frequently, and there is some evidence that the churchyard that inspired his poem was not, in fact, the accepted Stoke Poges, but Everdon. Walk in the churchyard at 'parting day' and see what you think.

The countryside around Everdon is idyllic and there are many beautiful places to visit. The walk we take here is superb, and shows Northamptonshire at its very best, especially in the late springtime, when the hedgerows are ablaze with wild flowers.

The route first passes through the valley of the almost deserted village of Snorscombe – only the manor house (now the farm), the beautifully restored mill and a cottage remain – before a long broad track leads on to the Knightley Way, Northamptonshire's first long-distance path. You then pass through the edge of the pretty village of Preston Capes before following the Knightley Way across fields to emerge at Fawsley Park, one of the county's little-known beauty spots and an ideal spot for a picnic. The route returns over Everdon Hill, the highest point for miles around, with excellent views in all directions.

THE WALK

❶ From The Plough, walk on the narrow road downhill, keeping the church wall on your right. Continue on the metalled track. Eventually, it goes through a gate, downhill and over a brook. At the gate after the brook turn right on the track to pass the beautiful Snorscomb Mill. Continue uphill on the track to the farm.

PLACES of INTEREST

Half a mile out of Everdon, on the road to Farthingstone, is **Everdon Stubbs**, 70 acres of deciduous woodland managed by The Woodland Trust. It is simply beautiful. Paths wind in and out of woodland glades and in springtime the carpet of bluebells is breathtaking. There is a small car park beside the road and an interpretation board. Do not miss it!

Three miles east is **The Old Dairy Farm Centre** at Upper Stowe. Here is a delightful mixture of crafts and creatures. Young children will love all the farm animals and pets, while adults may watch craftsmen at work or even buy Bond Street fashions. There are various shops and displays and even an excellent restaurant. Telephone: 01327 340525.

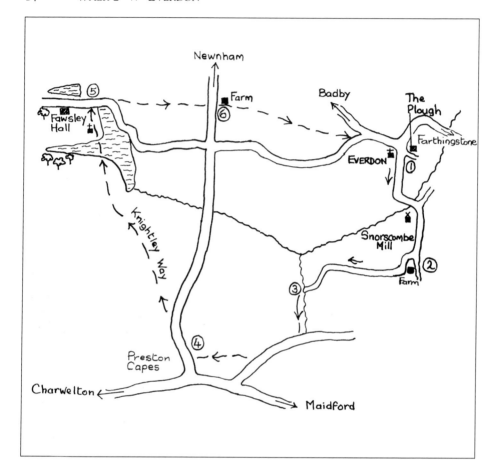

❷ Go through the waymarked metal farm gate, and straight on up the hill, keeping to the track around the farm buildings. Ignore the bridleway going off to the left at the sharp corner after the farm, and keep to the gravelled track for almost a mile, eventually bending to left and then to right before going downhill to cross a stream.

❸ Over the stream, turn left following the bridleway signs and cross a field to reach the narrow road. Turn right on the road, and in about ¼ mile, at the Knightley Way sign,

turn right across a field. Follow the Knightley Way signs directly uphill across the next field and head just to the left of the big house (a farm) on the hill. The Knightley Way reaches the road at the farm entrance.

❹ Turn right on the road, and at the bottom of the hill, leave the road again, following the Knightley Way signs across fields on the left. The signs and their direction are quite clear and you will be following them for some time. Eventually, you reach Fawsley Park and pass over the

Fawsley church.

lake and just to the right of the church. Fawsley Hall was owned by the Knightley family. The tiny church, which is always open, contains many memorials to them. Like Snorscomb, the village of Fawsley was abandoned on the orders of the Knightleys around the end of the 15th century, when the land was requisitioned for sheep grazing – a far more profitable venture. Later, in the 18th century, the deserted village was drowned when the park was landscaped by Capability Brown, who with his contrived informality created these beautiful lakes in this very natural setting.

❺ At the road to Fawsley Hall, turn right. You now leave the Knightley Way (it goes off on the left) and continue some 200 yards farther on the road, to where a footpath is signed at the top of a bank on the left. Follow the footpath across two fields to reach the road.

❻ Cross the road and in the next field follow the hedge to the top left-hand corner. In the next field keep to the hedge, and then follow the waymarkers across five small fields to where a stile leads you into the corner of a steeply sloping field. Here keep to the right-hand hedge to find a stile which leads you onto the road. Turn left and then walk through the village to reach the church and the inn.

EYDON

Length: 5 miles

Getting there: Eydon lies 8 miles south of Daventry on unclassified roads. It can be reached from the A5 via the unclassified road through Litch-borough or from the A361 by turning through Woodford Halse.

Parking: On quiet roadsides in the village.

Map: OS Landranger 152 Northampton and Milton Keynes (GR 543503).

Eydon's name is thought to be derived from the Saxon 'eye' – an isolated place – and 'dun' – a hill. And that describes it perfectly – a little village alone on a hilltop, miles from any large town, lost in the rolling countryside of west Northamptonshire.

But what a village it is! It is pretty in the extreme, but not with a chocolate-box, thatched cottage prettiness – the houses here are all of deep dark red local stone. The whole village has been a conservation area for 30 years, and no wonder – there just isn't another place like it! The view along the High Street is splendid, and when you reach The Green at the

FOOD and DRINK

The Royal Oak at Eydon is well worth a visit! To complement the atmosphere, the limited but varying menu is simply mouth-watering – try chicken liver, sherry and walnut pâté, followed by fillet of wild salmon with coriander and mango sauce! Telephone: 01327 263167. The Red Lion at Culworth is over 300 years old and is all beams and horse-brasses. The food is good and varied, with vegetarian options. Basket meals are excellent value. Telephone: 01295 760381.

If you are thinking of buying provisions for a picnic, there is a post office at Eydon which is also a shop, open on weekdays, and selling a few food items, including sweets and drinks. The village store at Culworth is open even on Sunday mornings and sells just about everything you could need.

end, you will find the stocks and whipping post and the old village pump. Behind The Green, a drive leads across parkland to the elegant Eydon Hall, built by Francis Annesley in 1788, while on one side stands the low 14th-century tower of St Nicholas' church.

Across the road from The Green, you will find the very old Wakelyn's Manor House, and just up the hill, the Old School House. Around the corner is the Royal Oak (with its attractive signboard) which has been serving ale for over 400 years. Inside it is bare and beamed with flag floors, almost a baronial hall in miniature, a very different hostelry. The house next door to it is dated 1652 and many others must be of a similar age. Before or after your walk, do take time to wander around and admire this little-known gem among Northamptonshire villages.

The walk is over field paths to the neighbouring village of Culworth. You first

descend to a pretty spot beside the River Cherwell and then follow waymarked paths through the fields to reach the village. In Culworth you pass the church and the site of an old Norman castle. The return is very pretty, with distant views of Eydon Hall on its hill. The way crosses a disused railway track and later passes through woodland and over a stream to reach the parkland belonging to the Hall. There are excellent views to the east and a good view of the Hall itself before you return to The Green.

THE WALK
❶ From The Green, walk uphill and follow the Culworth road out of the village. After passing The Old Rectory, take the bridleway on the right and keep straight ahead beside the paddocks. You will cross a track from the house and then come to a track at right-angles with a wooden field gate just across it. Go through this gate, across the field, and out at the waymarked gate in the lower hedge.

❷ Follow the bridleway alongside the field to emerge in another field beside the river. Here veer to the right past the lone tree and continue, keeping high above the river bank and heading towards the farm and a gate below the barn on the left. Cross the river on the bridge here and then head forwards and to the right to cross the river on a second bridge.

❸ Follow the waymarkers across two small fields, leaving the second at an iron gate beside a plantation of conifers. In the next field, head directly across, uphill, to a gap in the top hedge. The next field slopes

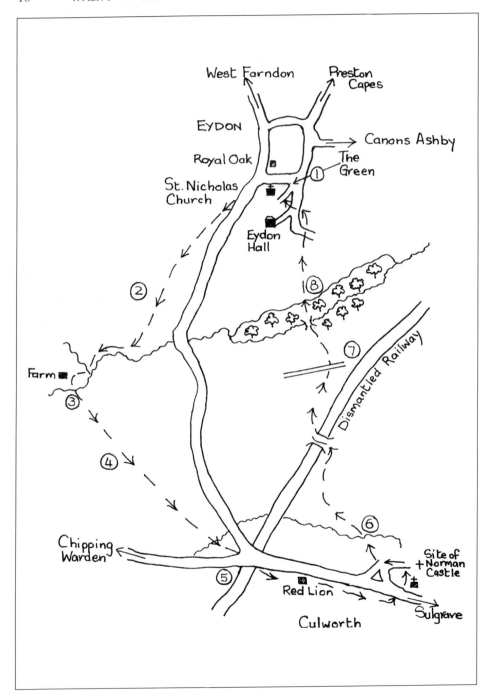

Wakelyn's Manor House.

gently downhill, and you should bear slightly to the right, heading for a waymarked gate in the lower hedge.

❹ Now follow the field edge alongside the next field and ignore a footpath leading off through a gap on the right. Continue keeping the hedge on your right in the next field, in which you climb and then begin to descend. A gap in the hedge ahead leads you into the next field where you keep the hedge on your left until you reach an old brick barn with newer extension. Follow a waymarked path diagonally across two fields to reach the road junction.

❺ Turn left and walk uphill on the road into Culworth. After passing the Red Lion, continue past the green to take a footpath

on the left just before the church. On your right you will see the remains of the Norman castle. At the top of the path, turn left and walk along as far as Fulford House Stables on your right. Here turn right on the footpath and follow the waymarkers down the hill to cross a brook to the right of a spinney at the bottom.

❻ The path now crosses the next field diagonally to a gap in the hedge on the left, but if no path is obvious you can follow the hedge around to the left instead. Follow the waymarkers through the hedge, across a small field and over the disused railway. Turn right and keep beside the railway to a gap in a spinney which is waymarked. Cross the field ahead in a straight line and then cross a track and, following

PLACES of INTEREST

Just 2 miles away to the east of Eydon, and likewise in the middle of nowhere, is **Canons Ashby**, a 16th-century manor house owned by the National Trust. There is much of interest inside and also fine formal gardens and a medieval priory church. Open March to November. Telephone: 01327 860044.

waymarkers, keep to the right of the hedge in the next small field.

❼ The next field is large, and the path goes straight across it to the woodland at the bottom. If the path has not been cut, you can always follow the hedge on your right without going too much farther. In the woodland, a waymark directs you to a bridge across a stream and eventually uphill to a stile over a fence.

❽ For some time you have been able to see Eydon Hall on the hill, and now you should cross the next field heading for the track to the right of it. Cross the stile on the far side of the field and keep to this track. Where it curves left in front of the Hall, go straight ahead alongside the wooden fence and then beside the copse and the pond. Cross the drive to a kissing gate in the wall on the left before the main gates. The path to your right now leads you back to The Green.

Stocks on The Green.

KING'S SUTTON

Length: 6 miles

Getting there: King's Sutton lies 2 miles south-east of Banbury. It is most easily reached by turning west off the A43 just	south of Brackley. **Parking:** On quiet roadsides in the village or on The Square.	**Map:** OS Landranger 151 Stratford-upon-Avon (GR 498363).

That Northamptonshire is the county of 'Spires and Squires' is undoubtedly true. Almost every village in these parts has its manor house and its church. Among the squires I would hesitate to choose, but for the spires there are surely two quite outstanding – Oundle in the north-east and some 50 miles away across the county in the south-west, King's Sutton. Here the elegant slim spire rises nearly 200 feet above the village and perfectly complements the landscape. At close quarters, too, its setting is idyllic in the lovely village square with its distinguished old buildings. As you stand by the White Horse Inn (itself more than 200 years old) looking towards the church, you have on the left the Court House, the oldest part of

FOOD and DRINK

There are three excellent hostelries in King's Sutton, and all within 200 yards of each other. The White Horse in the Square has a separately run restaurant which serves first-class food and is very popular for Sunday lunch. Telephone: 01295 810843. The Butcher's Arms serves meals lunchtime and evening, seven days a week, and has an extensive menu with particularly delicious desserts. Telephone: 01295 810898. The Three Tuns at the bottom of the hill was once three cottages and dates from 1680. This is a simple, genuine old pub, and the food here is good and certainly excellent value. Telephone: 01295 812685.

There is also a small supermarket for provisions near the school on the road to Warkworth and another small shop selling a few food items – and ice-creams – at the bottom of the village (down Red Lion Street from the church).

which dates from 1500, beside it the former Bell public house, now a fine private residence, while in the corner is the 17th century Manor House. The village stocks are on the green in front. On the right are the thatched old 'Monks Cottages', and next to them 'Lovells', a beautiful 18th-century residence.

It is well worth taking time to explore – look for the very old Q Cottage (circa 1550) on the road to the station! Before you leave the square, however, spare a few moments to look inside that lovely and interesting church. The story of St Rumbold is here – he was born in the parish some 1,300 years ago. Apparently he spoke, declared himself a Christian and asked for baptism (the Norman font proclaims itself to be 'associated' with this), all before dying aged three days!

The other story of the village is told here, too – it belongs to the eastern part of King's Sutton known as Astrop. Here in 1664, two doctors found a spring with waters which they declared – and, after a fashion, proved – to have remarkable properties, being good for just about every affliction. A well was built (and named after St Rumbold) and the well-to-do of the time came to stay in Astrop and benefit from its waters. There was dancing and feasting, card-playing, and a public ball held every Monday. Unfortunately, Leamington Spa became more popular and from the early 18th century Astrop was in decline. When Astrop House was sold privately some few years later, its grounds and the road to the well were closed to the public. The condition of sale was, however, that a replica of St Rumbold's Well, with waters from the same spring, should be built at the roadside where it would be accessible to all.

After passing the well, the walk climbs the hill through Newbottle Spinney to the isolated Newbottle church. It then descends through the charming village of Charlton with its interesting old houses. The route then climbs past Rainsborough Camp, an Iron Age hill fort with excellent views, and descends through the fields to the hamlet of Walton Grounds. Again you follow field paths to return, now with the exquisite spire of St Peter and St Paul's church to guide you home.

THE WALK

❶ Leave The Square, keeping the White Horse Inn on your right-hand side, and walk along Astrop Road in the direction of Charlton. As you are leaving the village, the replica St Rumbold's Well is at the bottom of the hill on the left-hand side.

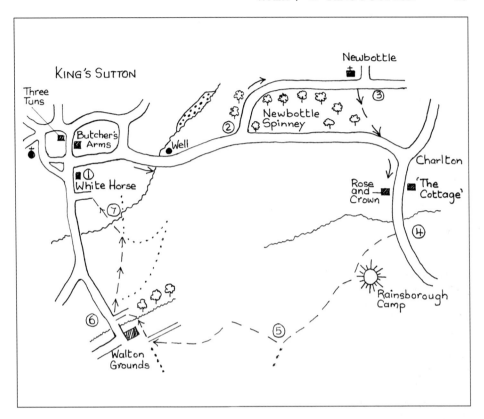

Should you be tempted to remedy a few ailments, you will find Northamptonshire County Council have added a small plaque: 'Water Unfit for Drinking'. How opinions change over 300 years!

❷ Turn left on the road through Newbottle Spinney, almost at the top of the hill. Through the spinney, enjoy the fine view to the north.

❸ Opposite the turning to Newbottle church, take the firm-surfaced path to the right. Where this meets the road in Charlton, turn left and later keep right into the village. Going downhill, you will pass the Rose and Crown Inn. Look out for The Cottage, once the home of F. E. Smith, Earl of Birkenhead, Lord Chancellor of England and friend of Churchill, whose country cottage this was. You can recognise it by the monograms on the drain pipes!

❹ Over the brook, take the bridleway on the right. After going through a gate, the path goes diagonally left across a field and then across a second field to reach Rainsborough Camp. The exit gate from the camp compound is on your right, although you may well wish to climb up and look over the rim before leaving. Through the exit gate, keep straight ahead

The church of St Peter and St Paul, with its impressive spire.

PLACES of INTEREST

Banbury, famous for its Cross, Cakes and Nursery Rhyme is just 2 miles away. Here there are some lovely old buildings (try following the Historic Town Trail) and a twice-weekly market. If the children need a treat after all that walking, try **Funtasia** on the Warwick road. This is a paradise for the under twelves. Open in school holidays. Telephone: 01295 250866.

with the fence on your right. Eventually the path passes through the hedge to run on the opposite side, giving excellent views.

❺ In the next field, the well-marked path crosses diagonally in the direction of a distant farm in the hamlet of Walton Grounds. It then follows alongside a ditch and across a field to reach a by-way. Turn right on the concrete track to the farm. Where the track bends left, go into the field on the right. Keeping the fence on

your left walk to the bottom of the field and then along to the right to reach a gate where you cross the brook. Head across the next field to the left, and then across another field to come out on a track in front of some houses.

❻ Where the short track reaches the road, turn right. After the houses, take the bridleway/footpath signed to the right. These fork after the first field, and you should keep on the footpath to the left, ignoring the bridleway going uphill. After crossing three fields, the path runs alongside a hedge. Ignore the path branching off over the field on the right and continue beside the hedge to the bottom of the field.

❼ Here cross the brook and follow the obvious path around the sewage works (well-concealed!) and over a final field to reach King's Sutton. Turn right on the main road to reach The Square.

MARSTON ST LAWRENCE

Length: 3½ miles

Getting there: Marston St Lawrence lies 5 miles north-west of Brackley on an unclassified road. Take the A422 Brackley-Banbury road and turn right in the village of Farthinghoe. It can also be reached from the B4525 which runs just north of the village.

Parking: It is possible to park on quiet roadsides in the village, particularly at the north end away from the church.

Map: OS Landranger 152 Northampton and Milton Keynes (GR 536424).

Marston St Lawrence lies tucked away in the quiet lanes of south-west Northamptonshire. Things were not always so peaceful! The road to the north, the B4525, known as Welsh Road, was the old drovers' route from mid-Wales to the markets of London. Marston Hill Farm, close to the road, was a popular overnight stopping place.

But well before the days of the drovers there was settlement in these parts. The Romans were here – there was a villa at nearby Thenford – and in the north of the parish a pre-Christian burial ground has been found.

FOOD and DRINK

Everything in Marston has a history and the Marston Inn is no exception. Originally it was taken from the church by Oliver Cromwell and given to the Belcher family. At some later date it became a butcher's shop, but now has been a hostelry for over 150 years. The food here is home-cooked and simply excellent, with a wide menu. The local dishes Chicken St Lawrence (in barbecue sauce with bacon and cheese) and Marston Chicken (with cream and Stilton) are highly recommended – as is the ham, eggs and chips on which the inn's reputation was founded. The baguettes, filled with anything you name, are fully two feet in length! Please note that the chef takes a well-earned rest on Sunday evenings and Mondays and that children may only eat inside on Sunday lunchtimes – there is, however, a garden with children's playhouse. Before leaving this remarkable old inn, ask to see Pumphrey – he has a history too! Telephone: 01295 711906.

The Inn at Greatworth is on the route and offers all standard fare, with some different dishes such as duck with honey and grape sauce or braised steak in Guinness. Telephone: 01295 710976. Also in Greatworth is a well-stocked village shop, should you wish to buy the ingredients for a picnic. This could then be enjoyed with a Cotswold view.

The church, too, is a place of antiquity. Its dedication to St Lawrence and the presence of an old yew in the churchyard indicate it may well have been originally a site of pagan worship. That yew tree is mentioned in the Domesday Book and certified to be over 1,000 years old. It is thought that the archers' bows for the nearby Civil War battle of Edgehill were cut from it. The interior of the church has many interesting features – and a booklet available to describe them. Perhaps most striking is the modern memorial altarpiece representing the Tree of Life topped by a cross formed from the nails piercing Christ at the Crucifixion.

Not far from the church is Marston House, for nearly 500 years the home of the Blencowe family. In the grounds are a shrubbery and lake, with an ornamental bridge dated 1759. Rather less conventionally, the grounds also contain the graves of three famous racehorses – *Reynoldstown*, Grand National winner in 1936 and 1937, *Well-to-Do*, Grand National winner in 1971, and *Nostrodamus*, 1981 Point to Point Champion – the house has more recently been in the possession of their owners.

The walk visits the nearby attractive village of Greatworth on those oh-so-quiet roads and so would be suitable if you wish to take a pushchair or other wheeled transport. One word of caution – Greatworth is barely 1½ miles from Marston, but is 130 feet higher above sea level. The climb up is gradual, but the descent is rather more dramatic! The views as you leave are magnificent. On a fine day the northern hills of the Cotswolds can be seen – and a bench has been strategically placed for you to view them. Sunset here can be a spectacle and when the sky finally darkens it is but a short downhill walk to Marston and the possible pleasures of its hostelry.

THE WALK

❶ Starting from the Marston Inn at the newer end of the village, walk along the main street southwards. After a sharp bend to the left you are in the oldest part and will pass the gates to Marston House, the 18th-century Glebe House with its circular dovecote, and the church with its yew tree.

The ancient yew tree in the churchyard at Marston St Lawrence.

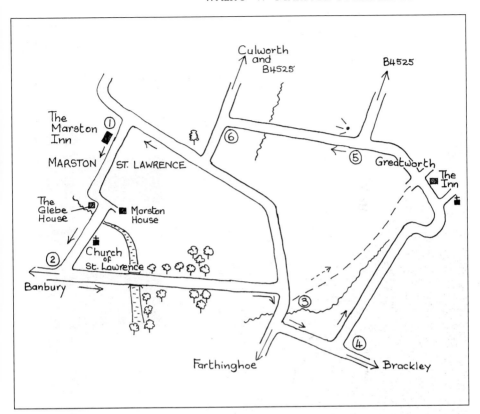

❷ Where the road bends right, turn left and follow the narrow road across the ornamental bridge and through the spinney. At its junction with the 'main road', turn right.

❸ Just before the next road junction (about 150 yards), a footpath crosses arable land to climb the hill directly to Greatworth, should you feel like some field walking. The footpath ends in a close which comes out in the centre of the village opposite the post office.

If on firmer terrain, turn left at the road junction just after the footpath sign.

❹ Turn left again at the next junction (signposted Greatworth) and climb the gradual hill to the village. The entrance to the Manor House is on the right as you enter Greatworth – the pineapple finials of the old manor house, destroyed by fire, are to be seen inside the present entrance. St Peter's church is in the next road along on the right, should you wish to visit it. Continuing on the road through the centre of the village, you now pass the pub (aptly named The Inn) and the shop-cum-post office.

❺ At the top of the village where the road

The church of St Lawrence.

PLACES of INTEREST

Three miles north is **Sulgrave Manor**, in the 16th and 17th centuries the home of the ancestors of George Washington, the USA's first president. Regular guided tours are taken around the house and there are also beautiful gardens, picnic facilities, a gift shop, refreshments, Washington exhibition, etc. Special event days occur throughout the year and you may find the building peopled with Tudors in costume or an American Civil War battle raging through the grounds. To experience – or avoid – these, and also to check opening times telephone 01295 760205.

swings right, carry straight on to the 'Road with a View'. Hopefully the weather will be suitable for you to appreciate it.

❻ At the road junction at the bottom of the hill go left. Turn right at the next T-junction to return to Marston St Lawrence.

SILVERSTONE

Length: 4 miles

Getting there: Silverstone is on the A43, 4 miles south of Towcester. The centre of the village is to the west of the trunk road.	Parking: On quiet roadsides in the village.	Map: OS Landranger 152 Northampton and Milton Keynes (GR 668442).

For many years the signs on the approach roads to Silverstone read: 'Silverstone – Please Drive Slowly', but eventually someone in authority spotted the joke and 'Slowly' was changed to 'Carefully' – an injunction perhaps more readily complied with in these parts! However, there is much more to the village of Silverstone than its racing circuit.

Silverstone was once a settlement at the heart of Whittlewood Forest. Forest crafts and logging were its way of life – even now there is a huge timber yard specialising in oak in the centre of the village. It is a very old settlement, appearing in the Domesday Book as Silvestone, and we know that by the 12th century the Plantagenet kings had set up a royal hunting

FOOD and DRINK

The White Horse in the centre of the village is a friendly pub with an extensive menu. The Sunday roast lunches are much sought after and the basket meals excellent value. Telephone: 01327 858550. The Royal Oak on the A43 has on its bar menu, everything from rolls to rump steak. It also hosts a very popular curry-night on Wednesdays, when the chef has an opportunity to exercise his particular talent – although you may be able to partake of this speciality at other times too. Telephone: 01327 857187.

Should the day be fine and you decide on a picnic, there are shops in the village to supply all your needs. On a sunny day, the picnic site in Bucknell Wood will make an idyllic setting for your meal.

lodge here. There is much evidence of the community in medieval times. The part of the village called Little London was apparently settled by Londoners fleeing the Black Death in the capital. But the plague was here too and the village of Charlock to the west was completely wiped out. Its remains can be seen on your walk. Another casualty was the community of monks at Luffield Abbey to the east. None survived and the Abbey fell to ruin. In the Second World War an airfield was built on its site and this was later converted to the present racing circuit. What lies beneath is commemorated in the naming of Priory, Abbey and Luffield Corners.

Today Silverstone is an attractive and homely village. At its centre where four roads meet you will find the village pub, two shops and the church. The latter is a relatively recent edifice, being built late in

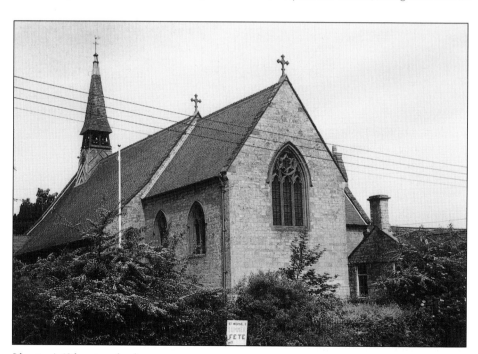

Silverstone's 19th-century church.

the 19th century and having an odd, rather Scandinavian-style spire. Further out are the schools, the village hall and the playing field – all the ingredients of good village life.

There are fine walks all around Silverstone. This one has been chosen for its contrasts of forest and open countryside. After leaving the Little London area of the village, the route passes the site of some medieval fishponds and then crosses two streams on wooden bridges. You then climb on springy-turfed grazing land, passing the deserted village of Charlock to reach the edge of Bucknell Wood. The wood is a treat at any time of year – bluebells in spring, rich colours in autumn and in between, the deep shade of summer or the silent snow of winter. You take a long walk through the heart of the wood, passing a superb picnic area in a clearing under the trees. The route returns to Silverstone on a long track that emerges from the woodland to give wide views of the surrounding countryside.

THE WALK

❶ From the White Horse walk downhill and continue straight ahead into Little London. Take the first footpath on the left between the houses. On entering the field, the mound on your right is the site of the medieval fishponds. Bear left across the field to the obvious wooden bridge on the opposite side. After crossing this bridge head diagonally for the top right-hand corner of the field where yet another bridge takes you across a wide stream.

❷ Over this stream, go straight ahead up the hill. From the top the abandoned village of Charlock is on your left (the farm

is called Challock Farm) and you can see ahead a corner where two hedges meet. About 50 yards to the right of this corner and well concealed in the hedge is a plank bridge over another small stream. This leads you into another field which you cross to the obvious stile at the top left. After this stile, turn immediately left and follow the hedge to the road.

❸ Turn left down the road and shortly right at the entrance to Bucknell Wood. Take the first track on the left about 20 yards inside the gate. This track passes a picnic bench near a totem pole and shortly afterwards emerges at a large picnic area with several tables. Cross the picnic site to the small car-parking areas. From the back of these several short tracks lead through the woodland to reach a hard-surfaced bridleway. Once on the bridleway, turn right and follow it gently uphill to the big track junction.

❹ At this junction, take the grassy track to the left, which is, in fact, a bridleway.

PLACES of INTEREST

Silverstone Circuit holds several events over the year. Unfortunately you cannot see the actual course when there is no event on, but huge boards inside the entrance gates display the coming programme.

Stowe Landscape Gardens, 4 miles south of Silverstone, are owned by the National Trust who proclaim them 'Britain's largest work of art'. In the vast grounds of Stowe School is a profusion of temples, arches, bridges and various other monuments by the most eminent architects of the Georgian era. Open daily in summer and approximately on alternate days for the rest of the year. Telephone: 01280 822850.

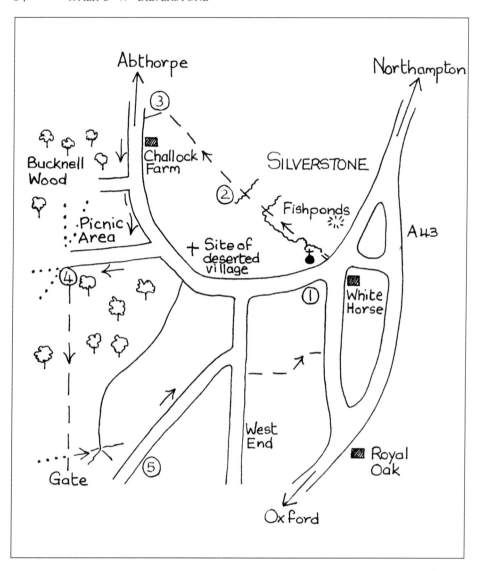

Keep on this track almost to the edge of the wood. Turn left at the track crossing just before the gate and in about 200 yards you come to the boundary of the wood with a stile on your right leading into a narrow field. Cross stile, field and another stile to emerge on a concrete road.

❺ Turn left and continue on the concrete road until it reaches a tarmac road at West End. Turn right up West End and take the first footpath on the left. This brings you out in the village just above the White Horse. Turn left to reach it.

GRAFTON REGIS

Length: 6½ miles

Getting there: Grafton Regis is situated beside the main A508 road, 9 miles south of Northampton.	**Parking:** On quiet roadsides in the village.	**Map:** OS Landranger 152 Northampton and Milton Keynes (GR 758468).

Grafton Regis is a village short on population but long on history. It all started when the Woodville (or Wideville) family arrived in the manor house, not long after the Conqueror arrived in England. Elizabeth Woodville's chance meeting with Edward IV (under an oak tree in the forest south-west of Grafton – the name Queen's Oak still appears on the map) led to their marriage in 1464 and subsequent seven offspring. The two boys were the unfortunate Princes in the Tower, while the eldest daughter, Elizabeth of York later married the Lancastrian Henry VII, so uniting Yorkist and Lancastrian claims to the throne and ending the Wars of the Roses.

Other monarchs were fond of Grafton.

FOOD and DRINK

The White Hart on the main road at Grafton Regis offers a variety of fare and a warm welcome – it declares itself a family-owned, family-run freehouse. 'Home-made' makes a frequent appearance on the menu and is applied to pasta dishes, pies, soup, etc. The baguettes with salad and a few chips are excellent value and justly very popular. Telephone: 01938 542123.

In Stoke Bruerne there is a great deal of choice. The Boat is an old establishment providing two bars, restaurant and the necessary grocer's shop for ice-cream. The modernised Navigation has interesting children's play areas both inside and out. The Old Chapel is a coffee shop, restaurant, picture gallery and craft shop combined, while Bruerne's Lock is yet another very fine restaurant. Between them they must cover all tastes and budgets!

Richard III stayed, and Henry VIII so much enjoyed himself here while courting Anne Boleyn that he bestowed on the little village the grand title of Regis. Elizabeth I stayed at the manor, and James I too, and in the Civil War it was a Royalist stronghold, eventually sacked and burned by the Parliamentarians in 1643. It was later rebuilt, the present manor house incorporating as much as was left of the old. Today it is a private hospital, a lovely old stone building standing beside the 12th-century church of St Mary the Virgin on the top of a hill.

The church too is worthy of inspection. Inside, you can see the alabaster-topped altar tomb of John Woodville and the many memorials to the FitzRoy family. Charles II – another royal Grafton enthusiast – bestowed upon his illegitimate son, Henry FitzRoy, the title of Duke of Grafton and his line survives to this day.

Besides the manor house, the church and White Hart Inn, there are only about 30 buildings in Grafton, many of them beautiful and very old thatched cottages. Enjoy them all as you set out for your walk.

The walk first crosses the fields to the attractive tiny village of Alderton. It then follows a bridleway to cross the River Tove, from where it climbs a low hill past the famous Stoke Park Pavilions to reach Stoke Bruerne with all its many attractions. Here in summer you can savour an ice-cream beside the Grand Union Canal while watching the succession of narrow boats working up the flight of locks and disappearing into Blisworth tunnel. You can eat in one of the hostelries beside the canal, visit the fascinating museum and browse in the shop with its painted canal ware. When you can tear yourself away from the scene, you return along the canal towpath, which you finally leave to climb the short hill to St Mary's church and the peace of Grafton Regis.

THE WALK

❶ From the church, walk uphill past the manor house and bear right at the fork in the roads. Cross the A508 and, ignoring the private track opposite, climb the bank to cross a stile into the field as directed by the footpath sign. Cross the field heading to the right of a line of trees where there is a gate with a waymark. From here follow the hedge on the left until you come to a waymarked post beside the hedge. Turn right and cross the field on a well-marked track heading for Alderton church.

❷ After following the waymarkers across two paddocks, you finally emerge on the

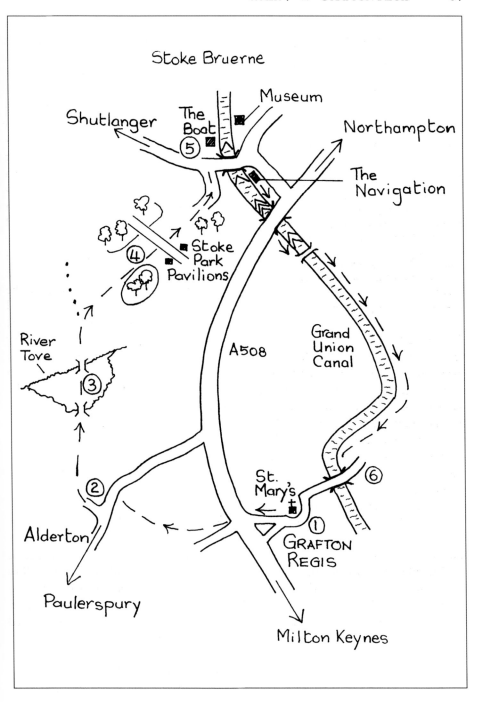

PLACES of INTEREST

The **Canal Museum**, fascinating and colourful, is open every day except Mondays in winter, while during the summer season boat trips along the canal start from just outside. Telephone: 01604 862229.

  Stoke Park Pavilions are passed on the walk or can be reached via the Stoke Bruerne to Shutlanger road. Designed by Inigo Jones, they were added to the existing manor in 1629 – their claim to fame is that they are the earliest example of the Italian Palladian style in this country. They are usually open summer weekends only.

---

road at Alderton. Turn left and then shortly right at the post box beside some thatched cottages. Follow this road which shortly becomes a bridleway and then joins a track to cross the stream on a brick bridge.

❸ Cross the field ahead aiming to the right of the barn. A plank bridge with rails takes you over the river. In the next field go through a gate in the right-hand corner and come to a waymarked wooden gate on the right. Go right through the gate and follow the well-marked route across fields to come out on a metalled track. You should turn right on this track if you wish to see Stoke Park Pavilions.

❹ To continue with the walk, cross the metalled track and almost immediately go over a stile on the left into the bumpy field beyond. Follow the waymarkers across small fields to reach an avenue of poplars – the old drive to Stoke Park House once went between them. Another gate leads you into a green lane between hedges. You will pass a small nature reserve on the right and follow round the edge of a field to come out at the canal bridge at Stoke Bruerne.

❺ A glance over the side of the bridge to the left will convince you of the merits of a break here! When you are ready to continue, join the towpath and pass under the bridge to walk alongside the flight of locks. The towpath crosses the canal twice along the length of the lock flight, but finally settles for the left-hand side and you can confidently follow it for a further 2 miles to reach the bridge below Grafton church.

❻ At the bridge you leave the towpath and cross the canal to climb the hill to Grafton Regis.

ROTHERSTHORPE

Length: 3 miles

Getting there: Rothersthorpe	west of Northampton.	Map: OS Landranger 152
lies 2 miles south-west of		Northampton and Milton
Northampton. It is signposted	Parking: On quiet roadsides in	Keynes (GR 714567)
from the roundabout at the	the village. There is a small	
junction of the A45 and A43	parking area near the church.	

Ask anyone today what they know of Rothersthorpe and you are likely to be told that it is on the M1 – or at least its service station is. A latter-day claim to fame! Some 200 years ago, a similar traveller might have told you that it was beside the Grand Union Canal. But let us go back in time just a few years more.

At the end of the 9th century, England was divided by yet another transport route, the old Roman road, Watling Street. The land to the south and west was held by the Saxons, to the north and east were the invading Danes. Rothersthorpe lay near to the divide. Alfred the Great had died, but his son, Edward the Elder, was an even

FOOD and DRINK

The Chequers at Rothersthorpe is thought to be so called because at one time the land belonged to the Priory of St James in Northampton and the monks collected the rent using a chequer board. It is a friendly genuine local, but unfortunately for those who have worked up an appetite, does not serve food. (Telephone: 01604 830892) However, a short drive of 1 ½ miles (crossing the canal and A43) will bring you to the pretty village of Milton Malsor. Here, The Greyhound (access from main road and centre of village by the green) proclaims 'Home-cooked food. All day – every day – 8 days a week.' Sort that one out! Telephone: 01604 858449. The Compass, a smaller hostelry on the back roads, serves excellent lunches on weekdays only. Telephone: 01604 858365.

There are no shops in Rothersthorpe (although Milton Malsor has a general store), so would-be picnickers are advised to bring their own food.

greater fighter, making it his life's work to push back the Danish frontier. One day in AD 918 the opposing forces met in a mighty battle centred on Rothersthorpe, at the site which is now called Danesfield Farm. Edward won the day, and the victorious Saxons were able to claim that tract of land which is the modern day Northamptonshire. So Rothersthorpe played its early part in the shaping of this county.

A short stroll around the village will reveal other interesting features from its past. At its very heart is a large ancient earthworks known as The Berry. Its obscure origins invite you to speculate! It may have been a medieval defence, but is probably from much earlier times. Also worthy of a visit is the church of St Peter and St Paul. The 13th-century tower has a curious saddle-back roof of a kind not

common in this country. The base of a 7th-century preaching cross suggests that this was a place of worship long before the present church was built. Another building of note is the 17th-century Manor House. In its grounds is a circular dovecote, large enough for nearly 1,000 birds.

The walk is along the Grand Union Canal and its Northampton Arm. This, too, has its part in history. In the great Canal Age at the end of the 18th century, canals had been built connecting the Mersey with the Thames, the Severn with the Humber. The Grand Junction (now Grand Union) Canal passed within 5 miles of Northampton, but the company would not sanction a connection to the town – too many locks were needed, too much water would be wasted. Northampton's shoe trade was failing and the town was effectively stranded. After many years of petitioning, and the stop-gap construction of a horse railway, agreement was at last achieved and the line opened in 1815. It was immediately successful. The shoe trade recovered, other goods reached the town, and within 40 years, Northampton had trebled its population. What would Northampton's fate have been without this 5 miles of canal?

Today the canal with its 17 locks is quiet, the few pleasure boats using it are heading for the River Nene and the fen-land waterways. When you reach the Grand Union's Main Line, the scene changes – in summer particularly it is alive with all sorts of craft and people. Follow-ing it for just a short distance before you turn across the fields back to Rother-sthorpe, you may well think along with Ratty, that here, at least, it seems that, 'There is nothing – absolutely nothing –

half so much worth doing as simply mess-ing about in boats'!

THE WALK

❶ From the church, head downhill past the Manor House. At the junction at the bottom of the village, turn right and take the footpath on the left a few yards further along the road.

❷ Cross the field diagonally, heading for the top left-hand corner where there is a

The village church at Rothersthorpe.

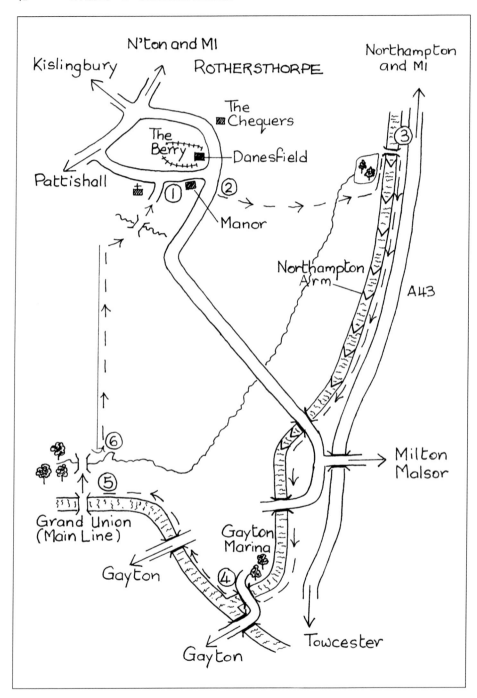

PLACES of INTEREST

Hunsbury Hill Country Park is 2 miles away on the outskirts of Northampton. The site is an Iron Age hill fort which in the 19th century was quarried for its ironstone. There is now an open-air museum in the old quarry with restored mineral locomotives running in the cuttings. The museum is open almost every day. Telephone: 0802 420985. An Ironstone Trail will lead you around the attractive site. A good place for a picnic!

---

the bridge just past Gayton Marina. Cross the bridge and join the footpath on the other side of the canal.

❹ At Gayton Junction, turn right on the towpath alongside the Main Line and keep to it as far as the second bridge.

❺ Over the fence beside the bridge, turn right and follow the track with the hedge on your right to the spinney and brook. At the corner of the field, some 10 yards to the left a plank bridge takes you over the brook. Now turn right and follow the brook for 50 yards or so to a hedge on the left.

concrete bridge across the brook. In the next field, again head for the top left-hand corner where there is a copse. (There is a track around the edge of the field if the path across is not clear.) Turn left between the copse and the canal until you reach the next lock which you cross on the footway on the lower gates.

❻ Here, turn left, and, keeping the hedge on your left, pass through two large fields. A third small field is then crossed diagonally to where a stile leads you out into a lane. Turn right and follow the lane to emerge beside the church.

❸ Turn right and follow the towpath of the Northampton Arm for over a mile to

PIDDINGTON

Length: 2½ or 3½ miles

Getting there: Piddington is 4 miles south-east of Northampton. Take the B526 Northampton to Newport Pagnell road and turn where signed in Hackleton.	Parking: On quiet roadsides in the village.	Map: OS Landranger 152 Northampton and Milton Keynes (GR 803546).

Piddington is usually heard of as the last of three sisters – Hackleton, Horton and Piddington. But, in this case, last is certainly not least, and Piddington well deserves some individual attention.

Way back in the Middle Ages, Piddington was the centre of the community and Hackleton a mere hamlet in Pidding-

ton parish. Then, in 1709, the new turn-pike road from Northampton to London was built passing through Hackleton and Horton, but leaving Piddington on the side. The village became a quiet backwa-ter, the main road through it remaining a track into the forest, and so it is today.

Strolling from one end of the village to

FOOD and DRINK

The White Hart at Hackleton is a friendly inn offering real ales and a wide variety of food. All the standard fare you can think of is here – ploughman's, jacket potatoes, steak and ale pie, pasta dishes, chilli, curries, scampi, chicken, steak, etc, while the 'specials' are chalked on a board. Three-course roast only on Sundays. Telephone: 01604 870271.

Just along from the White Hart is a village stores where the provisions for a picnic can be bought – or perhaps an ice-cream reward for after the walk!

the other, you will encounter several interesting old buildings – the stone Manor farmhouse, the old butcher's shop and slaughterhouse behind the red telephone box, the thatched cottage (the only one in the village) that was once the National school and the Wesleyan chapel built in 1851. The 13th-century church of St John the Baptist stands placidly at the top of the village. It seems to have had a tower/spire conversion somewhere over the centuries. Its tranquil interior has a striking recent addition. The exotic vestry curtain was embroidered by ladies of the parish over ten years, the work being completed in 1991. A nearby sampler tells its story.

This short walk is on well-marked and well-surfaced paths across the surrounding countryside with wide views all around. It starts from the church and initially follows a route which has been given the title The Old Deer Park Trail. You may still find deer here today. These, however, are the tiny muntjacs – descendants of those intrepid escapees from Woburn Abbey in more recent times. Returning towards Pid-

dington, the trail crosses the site of a Roman villa which has been undergoing excavation for 20 years. If you decide to take the longer route, you can then walk right through the village and come out on the aptly named Wet Day Path – a tarmac pathway running between the fields and over the brook to Hackleton. Here you may visit the White Hart Inn, the Carey Baptist Memorial Chapel or the perhaps seemingly unlikely combination of both! The route returns from Hackleton alongside the brook and climbs through a field to Piddington church.

THE WALK

❶ From the church walk up Church End and just past the junction take the footpath on the right signposted to Quinton and Preston Deanery. Follow the obvious track straight ahead to reach Preston Wood. The Old Deer Park Trail is thought to follow

PLACES of INTEREST

Salcey Forest, 3 miles south of Piddington, is a large woodland area managed by the Forestry Commission. Here there are car parks and Nature Trails (follow the woodpeckers!). There are also permanent orienteering courses – great fun if you have never tried it. Maps are available from Forest Enterprise, telephone: 01780 444394.

At Hardingstone, 4 miles north-east on the outskirts of Northampton, you can see one of the **Eleanor Crosses**. These stone crosses were erected at the end of the 13th century by Edward I after the death in Nottinghamshire of his wife, Queen Eleanor. They marked the overnight stopping places of her funeral procession on its route to Westminster Abbey. Originally 12 in number, three only remain – at Geddington and Hardingstone in Northamptonshire and Waltham Cross in Hertfordshire.

The Roman villa excavations, Piddington.

approximately the boundary of a deer park founded in the 13th century by Walter de Preston when he obtained a grant to stock it from nearby Salcey Forest.

❷ Just through the wood, keep to the hedge on the right and then bear left across agricultural land on a well-marked path. Should you be here at ploughing time when the path is obliterated, follow the direction on the waymark and aim well to the left of the farm. There are wide views to Northampton and to Salcey Forest.

❸ At the junction with the grassy track, turn left and follow the track to a signpost at the bottom of a dip beside a small group of trees. Turn left here and climb the hill towards the small spinney at the top. The path passes to the right of this spinney and then keeps straight ahead with the hedge on the left. After about 250 yards, a bridleway (Midshires Way) goes off on the right, but you continue to bear left beside the hedge.

❹ In about 200 yards, turn sharp right following the footpath sign to reach the hedge at the bottom of the field. You will cross the site of the Roman villa and should be able to see the current excavations. Only a little is visible now as that which has already been investigated has been covered over and returned to agricultural land. You will have to use your imagination to see the huge double-winged villa with courtyard, outbuildings and bath houses which once existed here. Turn left along the hedge.

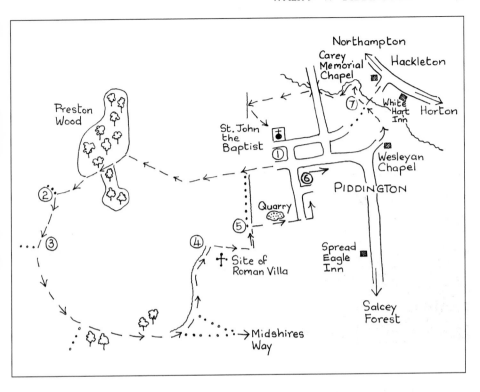

5 At a waymarked gap in the hedge, turn right on a footbridge across the ditch and cross the field. You will pass a wooded quarry with limekilns closed some 70 years ago on your left-hand side. At the road (Old End) turn left to return to the church.

6 If you wish to take the longer walk to Hackleton, bear right at the junction and follow Church Road through the village. Where Church Road bears right, walk up Chapel End and continue down the footpath at its end. Turn right on the tarmacked Wet Day Path and follow it to the main road at Hackleton. The Carey Memorial Chapel is on your left and the White Hart Inn 200 yards on the right. William Carey, founder member of the Baptist Missionary Society, was a cobbler in Hackleton before realising his calling and, in 1793, going out to India to spend the rest of his life there. He translated parts of the Bible into 27 different Indian dialects and indeed made six complete translations – quite amazing for a Northamptonshire shoeworker! He lived in Piddington for ten years and was married in the church there.

7 Returning down the Wet Day path, take the stile on the right just after the brook. The path runs alongside the brook to the lane. Cross the lane and take the footpath across the field. At the far hedge, double back to the left and take the broad track up the hill to the church and through the churchyard.

EARLS BARTON

Length: 4 miles

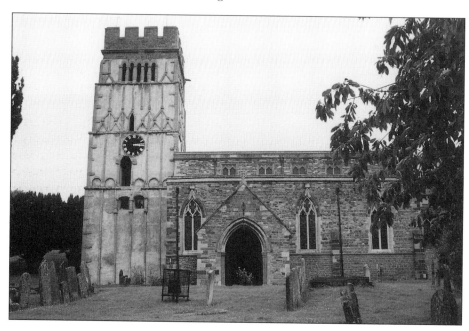

Getting there: Earls Barton lies midway between Northampton and Wellingborough and may be reached by taking either of the signed exits from the A45.	Parking: There is a small car park in the square opposite the church. If full, roadside parking is possible.	Map: OS Landranger 152 Northampton and Milton Keynes (GR 853637).

Hurrying by on the A45 from Northampton to Wellingborough, your glance may well have strayed to the north, where on a low hill sprawls a village dominated by an impressively large tower. There it stands as it has for a thousand years, the Saxon tower of Earls Barton parish church quietly watching over the river valley below. That church and its village are well worth a closer look.

Earls Barton is an old village. 'Buartone' in the Domesday Book, it acquired the 'Earls' later when it became the possession of the Earl of Huntingdon. Today it is a thriving community of some 6,000 people while still retaining its village

---

FOOD and DRINK

Earls Barton is blessed with a variety of eating houses – several pubs, a restaurant, a coffee house (belonging to the chemist's, and serving excellent meals during shop opening hours), a chip shop, an Indian take-away and a Chinese restaurant. But beware a Sunday lunchtime! Suddenly everything is closed and you are left with a choice of The Rafters, a well-recommended restaurant serving delicious three-course meals or The Boot Inn which confines itself to baguettes on that day. This may well be the day for a picnic – at least there are shops open for the ingredients – and you have a fine setting for it in the picnic area beside the river.

---

the 13th century but it was only recently – a mere 100 years ago – that Barker's of Earls Barton began making their fine quality shoes in the village. Their new factory is in West Street, close to the square, and adjacent to their factory shop is the Museum of Local Life. The square is the centre of life in the village and here you may sink on to a bench under the trees and ponder the changing scenes that tower must have seen through its many years.

The walk leaves the village following an old track towards the river. The route now follows the winding river, crossing from bank to bank along a very pretty stretch. On the hill opposite Earls Barton, another fine church tower (16th-century this time) dominates the skyline. This is Whiston church, and is the work of one Anthony Catesby, whose labour of love took him some 25 years. The riverside path traverses a pleasant picnic area and, in all, three locks are passed. The Nene is now becoming very popular with boaters, and on a summer's weekend you may well have the opportunity to be a 'gongoozler' – a boater's term for the folk who gather to watch a boat working through a lock! After a particularly attractive stretch with river on one side and lake on the other, we leave the Nene, passing an old mill house, and climb the hill to return to Earls Barton.

atmosphere. All Saints church stands at the heart of the village on a huge mound, Berry Mount, which was questionably once an Iron Age hill fort and almost certainly the site of a Roman 'specula' or watch tower. The present tower may even have been built along those lines. At any rate, it is an extraordinary affair, and one of the most important Saxon buildings in England. The elaborate stone 'ribbing' dates it fairly precisely at around AD 970 and is a feature found more commonly in Germany and Austria than in Britain. The vast nave is a Norman addition and the parapet was added in the 15th century. From the arched doorway beneath the clock the priest would have addressed his Saxon flock. He lived in the tower too, which he entered by a long ladder from the ground floor nave.

But what of the village below? The oldest surviving building is the 17th-century Manor House in the High Street, but there are also many other fine old houses. Shoemaking here can be traced back to

THE WALK

❶ From the square, keep the church on your right and climb uphill, following the main road past many interesting ironstone houses. Just before the road junction, turn left down Aggate Way following the Nene Way signs.

White Mills Lock on the River Nene.

❷ Following the Nene Way signs, cross the road. This is now the old Clay Lane – a footbridge was installed to carry it over the A45. When, in 1979, the decision was taken to allow gravel extraction here for the building of the A45, a hurried excavation was carried out. The small area of 30 hectares to the north and south of the road produced a wealth of Iron Age and Romano-British finds. The excavation site was on your right before and after the footbridge. After crossing the A45, continue down Clay Lane to the gate at the end.

❸ At this gate, bear right across the fields to cross the river at Whiston Lock. St Mary's church at Whiston is on the skyline ahead. Leave the Nene Way and turn left

PLACES of INTEREST

Should you be in Earls Barton on a Saturday, the **Museum of Local Life** (next to Barker's Shoe Factory) will make an interesting visit. The interior of a Victorian shoeworker's cottage is the main exhibit. If you are planning the trip on any other day, the friendly volunteers who run it are happy to open up for you. They asked me to include their telephone number: 01604 811735.

   Castle Ashby, 4 miles south, has many attractions. The house itself is not open to the public, but the fine gardens are, and there is also a farm shop and farmyard craft centre with a restaurant. Telephone: 01604 696696.

   Billing Aquadrome, 4 miles west, will provide you with entertainment of a livelier kind. Fun fair, boating lake, mini train, swimming pool, and much more are to be found on this site beside the river. Telephone: 01604 408181.

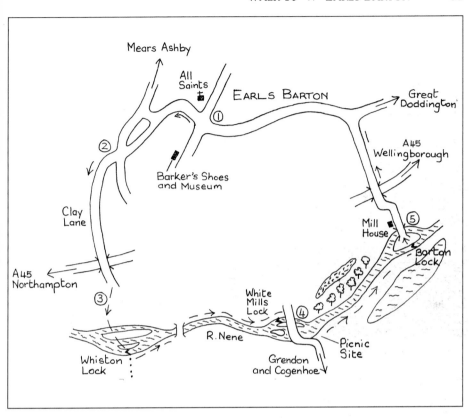

alongside the river. After a short distance, cross the river on a footbridge and keep to the opposite bank through several fields to the road at White Mills Lock.

❹ Turn right on the road and cross the river. Immediately turn left through the picnic area and follow the path alongside the river past gravel workings and out into the fields. Cross the river at Barton Lock, and again following the Nene Way, head towards the white mill house across the fields.

❺ Join the gravelled track and follow it up over the A45 and onwards to meet the main road on the outskirts of Earls Barton. Here turn left and follow the road back to the town centre and the square. Before you leave, walk uphill from the church 100 yards and take the track up to the recreation ground. From here you can see the deep moat dug into Berry Mount. Its origins are obscure – Iron Age, Saxon, Norman, medieval, all have been postulated. Feel free to add your own theory to the many in existence!

GREAT ADDINGTON

Length: 3 or 4 miles

Getting there: Great Addington is 7 miles east of Kettering and can be reached from the A14 via the A510, or from the A6 by turning northwards at Irthling-borough.	Parking: It is usually possible to park at the Memorial Hall opposite the church (unless there is a function on). Otherwise, park in one of the quiet cul-de-sacs in the village.	Map: OS Landranger 141 Kettering and Corby (GR 958750).

The Romans came to Great Addington. They built their villas beside the River Nene and the road joining their camp at Irchester to the east-west Gartree Road passed through the village on its eastern side. Was there a settlement at Addington then? We do not know, but there certainly was soon afterwards as Saxon pottery has been found at various sites in the village and in the 19th century a Saxon graveyard was found on Shooters Hill. The village is mentioned in the Domesday Book as Edintone and this region was then the most densely populated part of Northampton-

FOOD and DRINK

The tiny Hare and Hounds at Great Addington gets my vote for the most imaginative pub food in the county. The menu is not extensive, but it changes with the seasons and even the most prosaic-sounding dish is exotic here. The humble ploughman's is unrecognisable – no farm hand could contemplate an afternoon's labouring after this one! I will say no more, you must try for yourselves. But beware – these delights are only available at lunchtimes, Monday to Friday, so time your walk accordingly. Telephone: 01536 330661. The Axe and Compass at Ringstead (reached from lakeside) is an old pub which has been modernised and now has very good eating facilities. Bar snacks – which are everything from sandwiches to sirloin steaks – are served lunchtime and evening seven days a week (except Sunday evening). The home-made dishes are justifiably very popular. There is also a restaurant with a mouth-watering menu. Telephone: 01933 622227.

Following the road to the left past the Axe and Compass will bring you into the village of Ringstead where there are shops which can supply all your picnic needs. There are picnic tables beside Kinewell Lake.

Around the village is much evidence of earlier settlements – Bronze Age tumuli, Roman villa sites, deserted medieval villages, all within a mile or two. This walk passes some of them, but also has another attraction – on the hill above Great Addington is an excellent viewpoint from which you can see twelve churches – ten spires and two towers – along the Nene Valley. All are visible with the naked eye on a clear day, but a pair of binoculars will help! The route then descends to the river near Woodford and returns along the valley to cross the river at Willy Watt Mill, originally a paper mill in the 18th century. The mill wheel can still be seen. There is now an optional detour around Kinewell Lake – a flooded gravel pit rich in wildlife – before returning across the river and beside Brightwells Lake to Great Addington.

Take the walk at any time of the year – the paths are good. But it is at its best on a bright, crisp winter's morning, when the spires stand out clearly on the horizon and the Nene is a winding silver ribbon in the valley below.

THE WALK

❶ From the church, walk down the hill and at the Hare and Hounds turn left along the road to Ringstead.

❷ After leaving the village, as the road begins to climb uphill again, take the first footpath on the left. This footpath follows the route of the old Roman road. It runs around the edge of a field above a brook to reach a stile in the corner of another field. Over this stile, you turn uphill immediately to cross a second stile. Now follow the path uphill with the hedge on your right and

shire. Not so now! The villages here are quiet, but the 300 or so residents of Great Addington have all the ingredients of good community life – church, pub, school, village hall and post office.

The most prominent building in the village is the 17th-century Manor House. Sharp-eyed children will enjoy looking for the date carved in its long wall as you walk down the main street. Just across the road is a row of listed buildings – Carler's Farm, Ferndale, Manor Farm House and the Hare and Hounds, an 18th-century 'purpose-built' public house. The church with its fine Norman arch stands high above all at the fork of the roads.

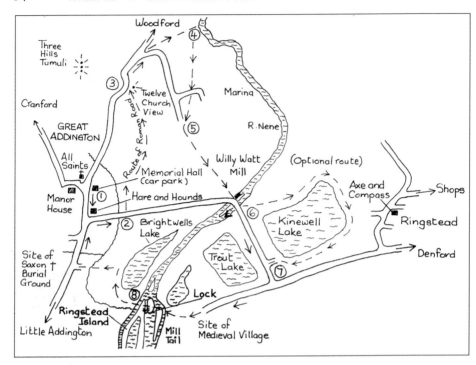

when you reach the top, cross the field ahead diagonally on the obvious path.

❸ Where the path meets the road, climb on to the bank and look around. From this point, twelve churches can be seen and it is hoped that in the future there will be a display board to help you identify them. In the meantime, an OS map will help. When you finally weary of those churches, turn right on the road towards Woodford. On the other side of the road you can see three low hills with a few trees on them – these are Bronze Age tumuli which have never been fully excavated. Keep to the road and shortly you will pass a concrete track leading off on the right and, just afterwards, a stile in the hedge. Cross this stile and the field behind it to reach another stile in the

bottom left-hand corner.

❹ Over this stile, turn right and follow the field path (now the Nene Way) over yet another stile into a field above the river. Keep straight on with the hedge on your right – you will be following the Nene Way almost back to Great Addington now. Cross the metalled track to the marina and then follow the way diagonally uphill across a field to come out on a long straight track.

❺ Turn left on the track and follow it across the disused railway and onwards to emerge on the road at Willy Watt Mill. Turn left.

❻ After crossing the river near the lock, you will see an entrance to Kinewell Lake

Water lillies on the Mill Tail, Great Addington.

on the left. You now have the option of following the obvious trail around the lake – at least around three sides of it – or going straight on down the road. If you choose the lake, it will take an extra half hour or so, but it is very attractive and there are waterside seats and a hide to view the birds. The route comes out on to the road again, near the sharp corner.

❼ At this corner, where the road turns sharp left, turn right and follow the lesser road past the trout fishery and on to where it becomes a gravelled track. In the field on the left once stood the medieval village of Mill Cotton. Passing through a metal gate, you arrive at a large clear area which was once the site of Ringstead and Addington Station. Following the gravelled track onwards, you pass the site of the old mill (as in Mill Cotton) and then cross the river

which is divided into several channels here.

❽ After crossing the second bridge, you should now leave the Nene Way and keep right around the shore of Brightwells Lake. Turn left on the broad grassy track that leads away from the lake towards the village. Keep straight on beside the hedge, and then turn left over the brook and uphill on the track to join the Addington Road. Turn right and keep straight on through the village to reach the church.

PLACES of INTEREST

Six miles to the west of Great Addington, on the outskirts of Kettering, is **Wicksteed Park**, a paradise for children (and selected adults!). Here you will find a wealth of playground equipment accompanied by a variety of theme park-like rides. Telephone: 01536 512475.

ALDWINCLE

Length: 4 miles

Getting there: Follow the A605 north from Thrapston. In about 2 miles, at Thorpe Waterville, take the left turn signposted to Aldwincle, which lies a further 1½ miles along the road. The village can also be reached from the A6116 Corby to Islip road.

Parking: On quiet roadsides in the village, perhaps best alongside the small triangular green area. Alternatively, there is a car park on Lowick Lane beside the Nature Reserve.

Map: OS Landranger 141 Kettering and Corby (GR 004820).

The Nene Valley below Wellingborough is quite enchanting. Those fortunate enough to be acquainted with our inland waterways will tell you it offers some of the most picturesque cruising in England. The Nene winds through a green and fertile land where at every bend stands a village of old stone cottages beneath a tall grey church spire. Aldwincle is such a village – indeed, its curious name derives from the Saxon 'wincel' meaning a corner or bend.

The village is unique in being composed of two parishes which were amalgamated in 1879. The parish church

---

FOOD and DRINK

There is no pub in Aldwincle, but there is an excellent village shop. Picnic tables are provided for an alfresco meal beside Harper's Brook, at the start or finish of your walk. The Fox at Thorpe Waterville is 1½ miles away along a pleasant road – you could extend your walk! The fare is traditional, but very well presented, and the range of ales is excellent. A log fire roars in winter. Telephone: 01832 720274. The King's Head at Wadenhoe lies 1½ miles away in the opposite direction. A small thatched pub, it is perhaps at its very best in summer when meals may be taken in the garden which slopes down to the river. Lunches are fairly simple – ploughman's, soups, etc – while delicious full meals are served in the evenings. Roast Sunday lunches are served in winter and are definitely to be recommended – for the end of the walk only! Telephone: 01832 720024.

Fuller, historian and divine, was born here in 1608. The rectory has since been pulled down but it stood in what is now known as Rectory Field beside the church.

The walk takes you through Titchmarsh Nature Reserve, an area of grassland, woodland and lakes created after gravel extraction here in the earlier part of the 20th century. It is an exciting world – alive with migrating wildfowl in spring and autumn, often flooded in winter, but on a bright summer's morning it is pure magic with the light sparkling on lakes and river and the warm air full of butterflies and dragonflies. Beginning your walk on grassy paths within the reserve, you return along a disused transport route. The line of the Blisworth to Peterborough railway, closed by Beeching in the 1960s, has here been used to create the Thrapston Town Walk, a well-surfaced track with pleasant views along the east side of the reserve.

THE WALK

❶ From the green in the Main Street, turn down Baulks Lane. At the junction with Lowick Lane, turn right. Turn left, following the 'Nene Way' sign (there is a small car park here).

❷ After crossing the bridge, turn right in the picnic area and follow the Nene Way alongside Harper's Brook. Some 150 bird species have been recorded in the reserve – if you have the time to stop in one of the hides en route you may be able to identify some of them with the aid of the charts inside.

❸ At the south end of the fishing lake

of St Peter stands in the centre of the village and boasts one of the finest broach spires in Northamptonshire, topped by a gleaming weathercock. The other parish church, that of All Saints, has a tower, and although the building is in good repair, it is no longer used for worship. It stands at the east end of the village close to the river and its pale stonework gleaming in the sunlight makes it a landmark visible for miles around. In Early English and Perpendicular style, it has a quiet beauty which attracts the amateur artist from far and wide.

The building across the road from All Saints was once its rectory but is now named Dryden House. It was in this house in 1631 that John Dryden, Poet Laureate under Charles II, was born and in this area that he spent his early years. Not being outdone, the rectory at St Peter's has also produced its famous scholar – Thomas

All Saints church, Aldwincle.

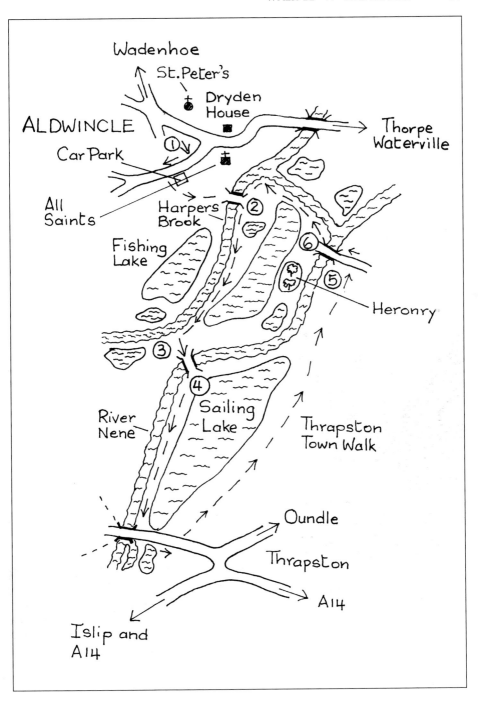

PLACES of INTEREST

Lyveden New Bield is about 2 miles to the north, although the drive (north on the A6116, turning right where signed) is about 6 miles. This is a remarkable building, now owned by the National Trust who keep it open all year. Designed and built in the shape of a cross around 1600 by Lord of the Manor and devout Catholic Thomas Tresham, it was intended as a monument to his faith. Unfortunately, Thomas Tresham died before the roof was installed, so preferably make your visit on a fine day!

Barnwell Country Park can be reached by returning to the A605 and continuing a further 4 miles towards Oundle. There are more beautiful riverside walks and an award-winning Visitor Centre here – see the entry under Polebrook.

well over a thousand years.

❹ Turn right and follow the gravelled track alongside the river past the sailing club. Turn left on the broad track and then take the footpath to cross over the bridge at the south end of the sailing lake. Turn left through a gate inviting you to join the Thrapston Town Walk which follows the route of the old railway line.

❺ After about 1½ miles at the end of the railway cutting, turn left on a wide gravelled track and cross over the river again. On your left, the patch of woodland beside the river was once a duck decoy belonging to Lord Lilford, but is now a thriving heronry where, at the right time of the year, huge nests can be seen in the tree tops.

(the one on your right), leave the brook and turn left on a wider track to cross a footbridge over the Nene. It was in this area during gravel extraction that the remains of the Roman bridge which carried the east-west Gartree Road across the Nene was found. The timbers of the bridge had been well preserved in the river bed for

❻ Turn right and walk beside the brook to the picnic field, from which you can retrace your steps into Aldwincle.

POLEBROOK

Length: 4 miles

Getting there: Polebrook is on a minor road 2 miles south-east of Oundle. It can be conveniently reached by following the signposted road from the	roundabout on the A605 just north of Oundle. Parking: There is limited roadside parking near the church.	Map: OS Landranger 142 Peterborough (GR 070872).

'Pochebroc' or Goblin Brook is the name of this settlement in the Domesday Book. But the goblins must have died out long ago for Polebrook is a very tranquil village today. Here, grouped around the lovely church of All Saints, is the most beautiful collection of old houses, each of local stone with a thatch or Collyweston slate roof.

Their names tell the story of bygone days in Polebrook – there was once a forge here and a blacksmith, a bakery and an old hostelry under a long thatched roof. Walk through this village on a sunny evening when the mellow stone reflects the long rays, and you are in for a treat.

The church itself is mostly Early Eng-

FOOD and DRINK

The King's Arms in Polebrook is a stone and thatch building about 200 yards along the road from the church. It offers a warm welcome – most especially so in winter when a huge log fire burns and the nibbles at the bar may include roast potatoes (excellent with ale!) The dishes on offer may sound fairly traditional, but they are beautifully served and presented and the salad garnishes are almost a meal in themselves. Main courses range from fish and chips to full Sunday roast, but there is lesser fare such as baked potatoes, baguettes and ploughman's, all offering the opportunity to sample that excellent salad. There are also starters, desserts and liqueur coffees to be added, should your walk have aroused a really hearty appetite. Telephone: 01832 272363.

---

lish, built around 1200, with a fine broach spire. Inside are memorials to the Ferguson family, relatives of the Duchess of York, who at one time owned the Jacobean Polebrook Hall, a short distance down the road. In the church too hangs the Stars and Stripes above a roll of honour for the men of the US 8th Air Force who in wartime were stationed nearby. Perhaps you should not leave the area without a visit to their memorial on Polebrook Airfield 1½ miles to the east. From this desolate spot regular missions into occupied Europe were flown by the brave men of the 351st Bombardment Group – among them the famous actor Clark Gable who was a rear gunner here. The book beside the memorial still proclaims almost daily visits from friends and relatives who wish to pay them homage.

The walk is an easy one, mostly on gravelled tracks and minor roads, but with some well-marked field paths. It leaves the village climbing a gentle slope to the east with wide views over Polebrook and Oundle with its tall spire beyond. The route then follows minor roads and a grassy track before reaching the hamlet of Armston, a once-thriving village which became deserted in medieval times. Onwards from here, the road leads downhill, and eventually comes close to the river. There is a fine view of the tall spire of Oundle church across the water meadows. A short field path now leads back to Polebrook, passing on the way fields which are winter quarters for various circuses.

THE WALK

❶ From the church, walk downhill in the direction of Hemington – see signpost. Approximately 50 yards after crossing the brook, take the footpath on the left. This

---

PLACES of INTEREST

For something original and different, make a visit to the **National Dragonfly Museum** at Ashton Mill on the road between Polebrook and Oundle. Unfortunately it is only open in the summer months, but then dragonflies are seasonal fare! Telephone: 01832 272427. **Oundle** itself, 2 miles from Polebrook, is an old-fashioned market town well worth exploration. The mellow old stone again dominates the scene and the buildings of the School are scattered throughout the town, interspersed with antiques shops and tea-rooms.

If you feel like more of the Great Outdoors, try **Barnwell Country Park**, on the A605 about ½ mile south of Oundle. There are lovely walks around lakes and river, while in the deservedly award-winning Visitor Centre (open weekends and holidays) you can hunt for mini-beasts and admire the remarkable array of fossils, all found in the park ranger's garden nearby. There is something for everyone in the family here. Telephone: 01832 273435.

The village pub.

hugs the woodland edge and the brook. After about 250 yards, where the brook makes a loop to the left, the path leaves the brook and maintains the same direction across the field on the right. The path should be quite clear, but if temporarily obliterated by ploughing, aim well to the left of the clump of trees ahead. Keep the same direction across the next field, and then across the corner of a third field to reach a deep ditch. Turn left alongside the ditch, and cross it on a waymarked footbridge just past the wooden barn.

❷ The path across the next field is usually quite distinct, but at ploughing time, head for the lone tree beside the hedge at the top of the hill. From there, cross the field diagonally left to meet the road at a fingerpost.

❸ Turn right and follow the road for about ½ mile. After the brick barn at a sharp bend in the road, there is a metal barred gate on the left with a track beyond. There may be no waymarking here, but you should go through the gate and follow the track for about 200 yards to a wooden gate on the right. This gate opens into a grassy field. Pass right through this field keeping the woodland on your left. Soon it opens out and descends to a gate beside a tarmacked track.

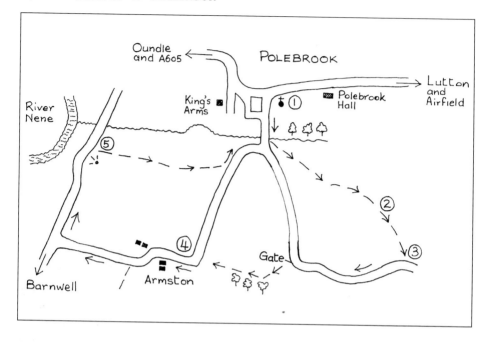

❹ Turn left and keep to this track through Armston and on to meet a minor road. (At Armston look for signs of the deserted village past the farm on your left.) Turn right on the minor road and follow it towards Polebrook.

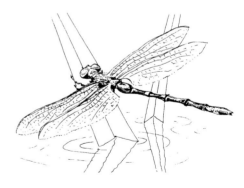

❺ Where the river approaches the road, turn right at a footpath sign – and from the bank, take in the view. Keep to the obvious footpath beside the hedges, passing the circus fields to reach Polebrook. On reaching the metalled track turn left and continue round the bend to meet the road. Here turn left and return to the church at Polebrook.

WALK 14

WOODNEWTON

Length: 4 or 6½ miles

<table>
<tr><td>Getting there: Woodnewton lies on an unclassified road 3 miles south-east of King's Cliffe. Turn left off the A605 road north of Oundle and pass through Cotterstock. Follow signs to King's</td><td>Cliffe and Woodnewton. It can also be reached from the A43 Kettering-Stamford road via King's Cliffe.

Parking: On quiet roadsides in</td><td>the village, especially near the church at the top end.

Map: OS Landranger 141 Kettering and Corby (GR 035945).</td></tr>
</table>

That corner of Northamptonshire to the north of Oundle is a remote and timeless land. Part of the ancient Rockingham Forest, once a royal hunting ground, the landscape has changed little over the centuries. Here large tracts of woodland still remain, separated by gentle farmland

and the winding Willow Brook. Woodnewton was one of the original settlements of the forest. Its old houses, built of the local limestone, stand quietly facing each other across Main Street, while the newer housing is hidden in Orchard Lane behind. Most of Main Street is a

FOOD and DRINK

The White Swan at Woodnewton is the only survivor of the original five pubs in the village. It has a small dining room with a bar area at one end and well deserves its recommendation by Egon Ronay. Here you may enjoy pan-fried duck breast with plum and gin sauce, sauteed pork fillet medallions and oyster mushrooms in cream and marsala sauce and many other similarly mouth-watering alternatives including vegetarian fare. There is also a fine range of home-made desserts. Telephone: 01780 470381.

The King's Head at Apethorpe is on the route and is a beautiful old building in keeping with the village itself. This is a family-run pub which offers a warm welcome to walkers. The bill of fare is again quite outstanding – even the bar snacks are a gourmet's delight, while the main menu (chalked on the backboard) proclaims such delicacies as rack of lamb with red wine, redcurrant jelly and mushroom sauce and rib-eye steak with cracked black peppercorn sauce, to name but two of many. Telephone: 01780 470627.

conservation area, and it is here that you can find the old manor house, the Wesleyan chapel now converted to a craft studio and the White Swan public house.

At the west end of the village stands St Mary's church with its features from the 12th century and just about every century since. The churchyard is managed as an area of limestone grassland supporting a variety of plants and wildlife. Here also is a surprise! Beside this very English church, far from his native Russia, is the grave of that great entertainer Nicolai Polakovs, Coco the Clown, who died in 1974. After his 'retirement', he worked for a time for Roberts Brothers Circus which has its base nearby, and he and his wife lived in Woodnewton. In recent years, Woodnewton has three times held a one-day Clownfest in his memory, and clowns from far and wide have been seen cavorting in the streets of this staid English village

The walk starts from the church and passes the very beautiful Conegar Farm, once an 18th-century water mill. It then climbs a gentle hill, from the top of which there is a fine view over Rockingham Forest. The path dips down to the forest edge where, if you are lucky, you may glimpse deer – at least you can find their footprints in the soft earth! After following the forest edge for a while, you climb slowly out of the valley and follow the metalled road to Apethorpe, a perfectly preserved estate village complete with stocks and whipping-post. You may then return along the quiet grassy-banked road to Woodnewton or, if you are feeling energetic, take the route to the north, some 2 miles farther. Your reward is a fine woodland path and from the top of the hill, a view over all the forest for miles around.

This walk is an easy one, and can be taken at any time of the year, but for a real treat, go along on a sunny day in autumn when the forest is glowing in colours of orange and gold.

THE WALK
❶ Opposite the church, turn down the lane signposted to Conegar Farm. Cross the picturesque bridge in front of the farm and follow the track on and up beside the hedge to the top of the hill. Here keep to the left of the copse, admire the views, and follow the well-signed track to the edge of the forest. Do not cross the footbridge, but turn right along the forest edge. Don't forget to look for the deer and their footprints!

The headstone marking the grave of Coco the Clown in the churchyard at Woodnewton.

❷ Turn right at a waymark and head away from the forest up the grassy track beside the hedge. At Cheeseman's Lodge, turn right on to the metalled road which is only an access road to Lodge Farm (to the left). Follow this for approximately ¾ mile to a four-way junction of paths.

❸ Turn right down the hill to reach Apethorpe at the King's Head public house. Turn right along the main road through the village. Only the occasional passing of a car will remind you that you are in modern times at this point! When you reach the church, a recess in the wall opposite is seen to house the village stocks and whipping post. On the right are the gates of Apethorpe Hall, which dates from the 15th century, but now sadly lies empty.

❹ Through the village, you cross a bridge over Willow Brook, with fine parkland belonging to the Hall on your right. Now you have a choice – return along the road approximately 1¼ miles to Woodnewton church, or turn up the bridleway through the avenue of trees on your left. Follow the bridleway through the forest to emerge at some restored farm buildings. Ignore the farm track to the road on your right, and continue ahead to reach the forest edge.

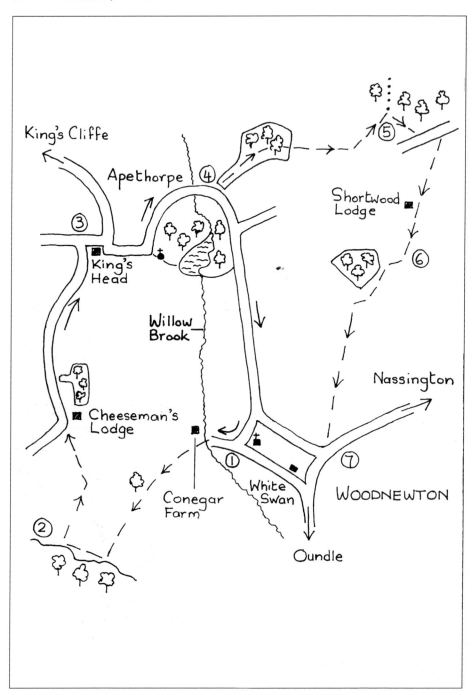

King's Cliffe

Apethorpe ④

③

King's
Head

Willow
Brook

Cheeseman's
Lodge

Conegar
Farm

②

⑤

Shortwood
Lodge

⑥

Nassington

White
Swan

①

⑦

WOODNEWTON

Oundle

PLACES of INTEREST

Wansford, 6 miles north-east, is the western terminus of the **Nene Valley Railway** which runs along the river 7 miles to Peterborough. The station is just south of the village, off the A1. There are trains (mostly steam) every weekend and some weekdays from February to November. Thomas the Tank Engine makes regular appearances and Santa Claus himself rides the trains during the festive season! Telephone: 01780 784444.

Stamford is 9 miles to the north. This very fine Georgian town is quite unspoiled and achieved fame as the setting for the BBC production of George Eliot's *Middlemarch*.

❺ Here go through a gate into the woodland and turn right on to a track which leads to the road. Turn left on the road, and after 100 yards turn right at the footpath sign. Cross the field to the hedge on your right and then follow this hedge on the field side past the training stables at Shortwood Lodge. When you have passed the house, a gap in the hedge leads you on to the farm track. Follow this up and over a stile into the field beyond.

❻ Follow the path to the woodland edge on the right and then turn left beside the wood. Where the woodland almost reaches a hedge, cross the field for a few yards, pass through this hedge, and then cross the corner of this field to go through an obvious gap in the hedge on the right. Now turn left and walk downhill beside the hedges on a clearly marked path with magnificent views and the spire of Oundle parish church piercing the horizon ahead.

❼ In Woodnewton now, turn right on the road and right again at the village sign. Walk up the Main Street with its attractive buildings to the church at the far end.

The village stocks on display at Apethorpe.

DUDDINGTON

Length: 3 or 6 miles

Getting there: Duddington lies at the junction of the A43 and A47, 4 miles south-west of Stamford.	**Parking:** On quiet roadsides in the village.	**Map:** OS Landranger 141 Kettering and Corby (GR 989008).

Duddington is delightful! One of the most attractive villages in Northamptonshire, it should not be missed – not that it could be missed once upon a time, as two of the busiest roads in the Midlands, the A43 and A47, crossed here. Now, however, they have been re-routed, and the village has been cleaned and restored to its former glory.

The roads, which lean down to the River Welland, are flanked by ancient stone cottages with Collyweston slate roofs, at their very best in high summer, when their gardens are full of hollyhocks and roses climb around the doors. It is a pleasure to wander here, and when you get as far as the river with its medieval bridge and old mill, the artist in you will cry out

FOOD and DRINK

The Royal Oak Hotel on the A43 is a very attractive and popular place. In summer, the outside floral displays are a feast for the eyes. Inside, the fare is magnificent. The vegetarian tagliatelle with asparagus sauce and baby sweetcorn is a popular choice – but a glance around the tables will convince you that all choices are delectable here. Telephone 01780 444267.

Regrettably, there are no shops in Duddington, so a picnic would have to be brought with you. You could enjoy it in the forest – there are picnic tables at Top Lodge – or perhaps go on to Stamford, where there is a lovely riverside meadow.

for brush and palette.

However taken you are with the scene at the river, do not leave without visiting the Church of St Mary, which was built in Norman times on an original Saxon site. From the outside you will see the odd position of the tower – stuck on to the chancel on the south side. When a tower was decided upon, there was found to be no room for it on the west side where the land falls away to the river. The south door is something to behold, with its heavy ornate ironwork. This dates from 1220 and was not merely for decoration, but for defence. The villagers could shut themselves into the church for protection against the marauding bandits of Rockingham Forest. Similar doors are seen on other forest churches.

Inside, the church has many interesting features. One that will immediately strike you is the curious 'curve' in the centre aisle. It is said that, when the chancel was extended in the 14th century, compass bearings were taken to find the East. But the 'East' had moved since Saxon times owing to the change in magnetic North – hence the 5° bend! What do you think?

Also in the church, you will notice the many memorials to the Jackson family. Nicholas Jackson in the 17th century was something of an entrepreneur. A baker in Stamford at the time, he began buying properties in Duddington. His son followed in his father's footsteps and soon the family became major landowners. Eventually they built the charming Manor House and set out its lovely riverside grounds – you can get a glimpse of it through the wrought-iron gates on High Street.

From Duddington, many excellent walks may be taken in the nearby forest. The Forestry Commission has its headquarters at Fineshade, and the woodland here is beautifully preserved with good tracks. A short walk is described, but if you feel more energetic, a waymarked 'red route' of about 3 miles will show you more and lead you past top Lodge where you can pick up forest information. Look out for deer – both fallow and muntjacs live here and are often seen. You emerge from the woodland at a high point with wide views over the Welland Valley before returning to Duddington.

THE WALK

❶ From the Royal Oak, take the footpath south along the A43 to where it ends (about 100 yards). Cross the road here (with care!) and take the broad gravelled track opposite, signposted 'Jurassic Way'. Climb uphill keeping to this track, eventually passing the Gas Valve Compound – where the track narrows –

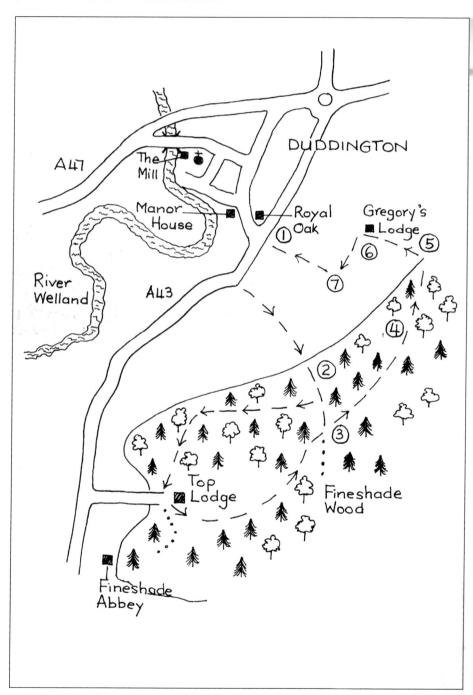

The old water mill at Duddington.

and then the barrier into Forestry Commission land. Continuing upwards, shortly after this a broad gravelled track branches off uphill on the right. If you are taking the shorter walk carry straight on to a four-way crossing of tracks (and point 3 below).

❷ If you wish to take the 3-mile extension, turn right on this side track and in about 250 yards you will come to the first 'red route' post – a green post with two red bands. You then follow this main track, and the frequent posts, for about 3 miles, passing Top Lodge and its caravan site when you are about half way round. After Top Lodge, the red route passes forest workers' cottages and climbs uphill, eventually turning sharp left on to a grassy track. At this turning, you leave the red route and continue straight ahead to reach a crossing of tracks.

❸ If you have taken the extension route, at this crossing you should go straight over. Coming from the main route (omitting paragraph 2), you should turn left at the track crossing. You are now on a gravelled track.

❹ After a while, the gravelled surface ends and the track becomes grassy. Continuing on this grassy track which bends left, you reach a broad clearing in the forest. Head straight across the clearing to reach a much narrower grassy track. Following this for a few hundred yards brings you to a gate at the forest edge.

PLACES of INTEREST

For more active enjoyment of the forest, you could try one of the permanent orienteering (wayfaring) courses set out in **Wakerley Great Wood** on the opposite side of the A43 from Fineshade and Top Lodge. Maps and instructions are available from the headquarters at Top Lodge. Cycling tracks are marked out in Fineshade Wood and again there are leaflets at Top Lodge.

The town of **Stamford** is a mere 3 miles north of Duddington. You can admire the splendid medieval and Georgian architecture or picnic by the river!

❺ Turn left on the footpath in the direction shown by the waymark (there are wonderful views of the Welland Valley). This leads to a small cleared area at the corner of a field where once stood Gregory's Lodge.

❻ From here, take the broad track which leads downhill towards the distant River Welland. At the end of the first field, the track continues ahead, but you should turn left on the track which branches off here.

❼ After one field, the track swings right and heads downhill again. Continue straight ahead and finally reach the A43 and the Royal Oak.

The bridge over the River Welland, Duddington.

GRETTON

Length: 6 miles

Getting there: Gretton lies 2 miles north of Corby on minor roads. It can be reached from the A6003 Corby–Uppingham road by turning right at the	bottom of Rockingham hill, where it is signposted. **Parking:** On quiet roadsides in the village.	**Map:** OS Landranger 141 Kettering and Corby (GR 900943).

Perched high on its limestone ridge above the River Welland, Gretton is a village with a view! To get the best of it, you should walk through the lovely old churchyard and lean over the grey stone wall. Below you winds the River Welland, and on its distant shore lies the proudly reinstated County of Rutland. A little

closer to home, the humps and hollows in the field on the right beside and below you mark the site of a former manor house. Its medieval owners must have enjoyed the view, too.

Gretton is one of the ancient settlements of Rockingham Forest. Its history, though, has been shaped by the deposits of

FOOD and DRINK

The Hatton Arms on Arnhill Road is the oldest of the three pubs. Its first landlord in 1672 was the black servant of Sir Christopher Hatton who had been given a lifetime pension after saving his master's life in a fire. The meals here are very good value, but are served only on Friday and Saturday evening and Sunday lunchtime (when traditional lunch is also available). Telephone: 01536 770268. The Talbot, in the centre of the village, was originally a farmhouse. It serves rolls, pie and chips, etc on weekday lunchtimes only. Telephone: 01536 771609. The Blue Bell at the other end of the village in High Street has preserved its character over the years. Drinks only are served. (Telephone: 01536 770404)

iron ore found in the local stone. Iron currency bars from the Iron Age have been found here and we know that the ore was quarried from Roman times until the Middle Ages. More recently, in the early part of the 20th century, one Samuel Lloyd came to live in the village, and it was he who set up the furnaces in Corby and made the first cast of pig-iron there in 1910.

The winding narrow streets of Gretton will reveal a wealth of lovely old stone houses if you have time to explore – not to mention the three hostelries, each of which has its story. At the centre of the village, below the green, stands the Church of St James, and it seems rather strange with its brown ironstone tower and grey limestone nave. Dating from the 11th century, it has fine Norman arches and an unusual 'distorted' east window.

It is from the church that the walk begins. It is a superb one, and particularly so on a hot summer's day when for some time you walk in the cool shade of the forest edge. The route passes Kirby Hall, possibly the finest Elizabethan house in the country. Farther on, you walk on quiet roads with distant views and then follow the Jurassic Way as it crosses between tracts of forest to emerge in the fields before Gretton. One word of caution – some of the stiles before you reach Kirby Hall are 'stock-proof', which also means 'dog-proof' unless your canine companion is an agility champion or of a variety small enough to be lifted over!

THE WALK

❶ From the green, walk up High Street away from the church, and immediately turn right into Caistor Road. At its end, turn left and immediately right down Southfields Road to where it becomes a track at the end. Continue straight ahead on this track for about ½ mile, ignoring other tracks coming in on left and right.

❷ After passing Kirby Hall Farm on the left, the track becomes unsurfaced and a

PLACES of INTEREST

Kirby Hall lies south-east of Gretton, about 2 miles away by footpath and twice as far by road. Almost totally ruined at one time, it has now been lovingly restored and there is much to see – and hear about, if you decide to take your own individual tour with headphones. Telephone: 01536 203230.

Three miles south-west of Gretton, high above the Welland Valley, is 1,000 year old **Rockingham Castle**. Teeming with history and legend, and riddled with stories of ghosts and buried treasure, a visit is a must! Telephone: 01536 770240.

Three miles on past Rockingham Castle is **East Carlton Country Park**, where as well as enjoying more walks, you can visit the Steel Heritage Centre which displays the history of the industry.

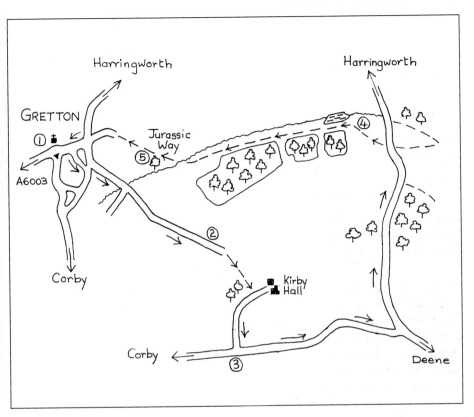

barrier prevents traffic proceeding. Continue straight on past the barrier to a field gate at the end of the track. Walk down the field with the hedge on your right. At the bottom, a series of four stiles leads you into the next field. Cross this field diagonally towards a gap in the high hedge at the top of the hill. Cross the stiles here and walk down the field to come out at the gates of Kirby Hall. Turn right along the drive and follow it left past the car park and on to the road at its end.

❸ Turn left, and follow the road for approximately 1 mile to its junction with the Harringworth road. Turn left in the direction of Harringworth and for the next 1½ miles enjoy this very quiet and scenic road. After a bridleway going off on the right, another bridleway crosses the road. Go left on this and cross the field towards the woodland. At the field gate, cross the next small field to another gate opposite, where you meet a gravelled track from the farm on the right.

❹ Turn left on this track. You are now on the Jurassic Way and will follow it back to Gretton. The Jurassic Way passes several blocks of woodland and then continues ahead where the gravelled track goes right. Shortly afterwards, you are directed right

Elizabethan Kirby Hall.

and then left alongside more woodland, and then right over a stream. When you reach the field, cross it diagonally to the top left-hand corner.

❺ Follow the Jurassic Way signs into the next field and then diagonally across it. The waymarkers then lead you across two more fields to arrive at a farm track. Turn right on this to reach the road. At the road, go right and immediately left along High Street. Passing the 18th-century Gretton House on your right, you return to the green.

ASHLEY

Length: 8½ miles, with short 2½ mile alternative

Getting there: Ashley is 2 miles north of the A427 Corby-Market Harborough road. Leave the main road at Stoke Albany, following signs to Ashley.	**Parking:** On quiet roadsides in the village, perhaps in Hall Lane near the church.	**Map:** OS Landranger 141 Kettering and Corby (GR 794910).

Nestling close to the northern borders of the county, Ashley is a little-known gem among Northamptonshire villages. The surprise here is that the heart of this village was designed by the architect George Gilbert Scott, otherwise famous for the rather better-known Albert Memorial and St Pancras railway station! Scott was the friend of the Rev Richard Pulteney, rector and squire of Ashley from 1853 to 1874. Scott was invited to redesign the interior of the 13th-century church of St Mary – the result you must see for yourselves. He also designed the old school with the attached master's house (opposite the church) and the many 'model' cottages along Main

FOOD and DRINK

The George at Ashley is a friendly pub, welcoming to walkers, with a very flexible menu where 'home-made' makes a frequent appearance. All food is fresh (they tell me only chips and peas are frozen!) and, as well as standard fare, there is an appealing 'specials' board. Telephone: 01858 565881.

Two other pubs are also on your route. The White Horse at Stoke Albany is well known for its excellent snacks and attractive meals. Telephone 01858 535268. The Fox at Wilbarston also serves a good range of fare. Telephone: 01536 771270. There are also shops in Wilbarston.

Street which are obviously in his Victorian Gothic style.

Although it may seem that the Rev Pulteney's hand has been laid on most of the village, there are older houses too. Ashley Court – originally the rectory until 1926 – was built around 1650, although the projecting part was added in the 19th century. Brown Horse Cottage and Yeomans in Green Lane are of a similar age. Shaw's Cottage, also in Green Lane, was perhaps a century later, and was for a time used as a dissenters' late night secret meeting house – they wished to avoid the rector's displeasure! The George Inn itself is 18th-century, and is the sole survivor of five inns in the village at that time.

A pleasant morning could easily be spent admiring the buildings of Ashley, but you must make time – and quite a lot of time – for an excellent walk. At 8½ miles, this is the longest walk in the book, but also my favourite! It will well repay your effort, though a shorter alternative is offered. The way is largely on field paths, but they are well marked out and for much

of the time you follow sections of the Mid-shires Way and the Jurassic Way. There is much climbing – and much descending. But the views are excellent, and changing all the time as you move from ridge to ridge. At times you have distant views almost 360° around you, at others you can see 7 or 8 miles up the Welland Valley or catch glimpses of Rockingham Castle, 5 miles away to the east. Spire-counting is a Northamptonshire pastime, and you have plenty of opportunity here. How many can you see at any one time? Take your time, your picnic and your binoculars and enjoy this most exhilarating of Northamptonshire walks!

THE WALK

❶ From the church, walk west towards the junction with the road to Stoke Albany. At the junction, take the bridleway signposted to Sutton Bassett and Great Bowden. Keep to this bridleway uphill through fields where eventually it bears left at a cross hedge towards a line of pylons. Under the pylon line, go through a small gate and cross the next field (called Five-Ways Field) diagonally to the right-hand side where you will find a rather stylish signpost. This actually offers you six ways.

❷ If you are just taking the short stroll, you should take the immediately left Stoke Albany direction from this signpost. This will take you out of the field through a gate on the left. Crossing two fields, you arrive at a gate at the bottom right-hand corner which opens on to a stony track. This leads down to the Stoke Albany road, where you turn left to return to Ashley.

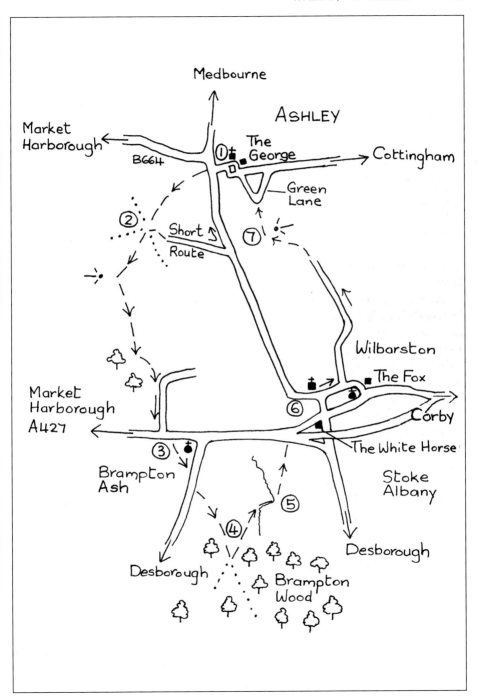

The church of St Mary with its contrasting stones.

Those out for the long walk should take the Midshires Way to Brampton Ash direction from the signpost. There is a wide view across the Welland Valley to the right. Following the Midshires Way signs, go through a gate at the top right-hand corner of the field and then, where the land begins to fall away, go through a gate on the left. Keep to the waymarked route across the valley and uphill across a small field. Turn left, following the waymarks along the field edge. At a gravelly junction, turn right uphill on a grassy track. Follow this to the A427.

❸ Walk 50 yards to the left and cross the A427 to the footpath opposite. Still on the Midshires Way, follow the route across fields, passing the attractive church at Brampton Ash and continue on to the minor road. Turn right on the road, and in about ¼ mile, left on the bridleway. Pass right of the farm buildings known as Red Hovel, and continue uphill following the signs.

❹ At the edge of Brampton Wood, turn left (the arrows indicate just about every other direction!) on the Jurassic Way, which you will now follow to beyond Stoke Albany. Follow the woodland edge for some distance to the very bottom of the hill. Here a waymarked stile on the right leads you over a stream on two footbridges.

❺ Cross the next field going uphill and head for the gate near the top right-hand corner. Cut across the corner of the next

PLACES of INTEREST

Four miles south-west, through Stoke Albany, is **East Carlton Country Park**. There are not only more good walks here, but an imaginative display featuring the history of the local iron and steel industry. Children will love the large play area with sandpit and the open grassy spaces amid the huge steel relics of the industry. There are also craft workshops and a cafe open all year. **Rockingham Castle**, seen from your walk, is 5 miles east of Ashley. See the entry under Gretton.

field to a waymarked gate and then head for a stile in the top right-hand corner of the next large field. Over this stile, head straight across the next field to a stile above the A427. Walk down the steps and alongside the A427 on the slip road. Turn left and, under the bridge, go on to the crossroads with the White Horse on your left. Cross straight over and go on down Ashby Road (look on your right for the 15th-century manor house) to The Green.

❻ At The Green, turn right to Wilbarston. Going uphill beside Wilbarston church, turn left on to a bridleway. Follow this for something over a mile, and at its end, cross the stream and head diagonally left over the field to a gap in the hedge. Maintain the same direction across a second field to a gate in the top left-hand corner. Here you are on top of the world with fine views all around. Try spire counting!

❼ Keeping the hedge on your right, descend to the farm and continue ahead on the gravelled track. Turn left at the lane to return to Ashley.

WELFORD

Length: 4½ miles

Getting there: Welford lies on the A5199, 2 miles north of its junction with the A14.	**Parking:** On quiet roadsides in the village. There is also a small car park on the Naseby road.	**Map:** OS Landranger 140 Leicester and Coventry (GR 642804).

The road from Northampton to Leicester winds quietly through Welford. The M1 has taken much of its former traffic and the village is quite a peaceful place today. Things were not always so.

Although a very much older village, Welford had its heyday in the coaching era of the late 1700s. Midway between the two county towns, it became a resting place for coaches and an overnight halt for

those going farther afield. As many as seven inns thrived along the High Street, and we can imagine the noisy scene with the constant comings and goings, wheels and hooves clattering and posthorns blaring. Even today three of the inns remain. A little later, in 1814, the Grand Union Canal was linked by an arm to Welford, bringing more travellers and yet another inn at the wharf.

FOOD and DRINK

The Elizabethan Restaurant in the High Street is not as formal as perhaps it sounds! It is a friendly place, very welcoming to walkers. There is a bar menu, a lunch menu and a restaurant menu – between them they must cater for your needs. The restaurant prides itself on 'High class traditional English food'. Telephone: 01858 575311. Also in the High Street is the Shoulder of Mutton, a lovely 17th-century inn, all beams and brasses. There is a wide menu, from ploughman's to steak, but the vegetarian options mushroom stroganoff and Raj vegetable curry seem attractive. Telephone 01858 575375). The Swan at the bottom of the High Street, is much more of a genuine local, and serves only drinks. Telephone: 01858 575481. Down by the canal, the Wharf Inn serves food from 12 noon to 9pm every day. The fare is standard, but excellent value and well-presented. The basket meals are very popular. Telephone 01858 575075.

Welford still boasts a post office and shop in the High Street which should cater for all your picnic needs. At North Kilworth narrow boats base, ice-cream and drinks are on sale during the cruising season. Telephone: 01858 880484.

casualty of Henry VIII's dissolution, but the site is quite prominent and well-preserved. Apparently a secret passage links church and abbey. You could seek it if you wish to view the site, but you would probably do better to settle for the field path. Beware though – ghostly sounds have been heard in these fields, apparently echoing from the tunnel beneath!

Welford is an excellent walking centre and there are many good paths going out in all directions. The Jurassic Way passes through the village and you can certainly walk to Sulby Abbey along footpaths. The walk chosen here, though, begins alongside the Welford Arm of the canal. This is a particularly pleasing stretch – narrow and reed-fringed, in summer the banks abound with wild flowers and dragonflies. When you reach the Grand Union itself, the colourful narrowboats claim your

PLACES of INTEREST

Naseby, the scene of the great and decisive Civil War battle of 1645, lies 3 miles south-east of Welford. The village itself is very pretty, and there are two inns serving good food, but the actual battle took place north of the village. To confuse you, there are two monuments some distance apart, both claiming to stand on the battle site. The first is an obelisk on the Market Harborough road, erected by the Fitzgerald family in 1823, but there is no doubt their siting was well wide of the mark! Eventually, in 1936 a monument was placed near the Sibbertoft road, on the ridge from which Cromwell led his army, and now a display board tells the tale. You can look over the valley to Dust Hill, where the king's troops were massed, and imagine the scene that summer morning! Should you be in Naseby on a Bank Holiday Sunday or Monday, you can find out a lot more about this battle at the **Naseby Farm Museum** on the Cottesbrooke road.

In the church, you can still see the travellers' chest, a huge old wooden box with three locks. The vicar and two churchwardens each had a key and they would all be summoned when a wealthy traveller was staying overnight and wished to place valuables in the chest for safe keeping. The church has many other interesting relics, not least of which is the 15th-century table tomb with notches in the edge said to be made by Cromwell's soldiers sharpening their swords before the Battle of Naseby.

St Mary's church itself dates from the 13th century and was originally a chapel of ease of the nearby Sulby Abbey. The abbey is there no longer, having been a

The scene of the Battle of Naseby.

attention. Soon you leave the canal on a wide grassy track which climbs gently uphill giving fine views of Stanford reservoir and the winding waterway below. Distant views of Welford itself guide you as you return.

is the infant River Avon, which rises in nearby Naseby and rapidly becomes the impressive river we know at Stratford.

THE WALK

❶ From the church, walk downhill along West Street (away from West End). It eventually bends right and joins the main road. Here you turn left and follow the road over the bridge to the Wharf public house.

❷ Turn left across the car park or down the short road to reach the canal. Walk along the towpath (which changes sides) for approximately 1½ miles enjoying the rural watery scene. On the other side of you

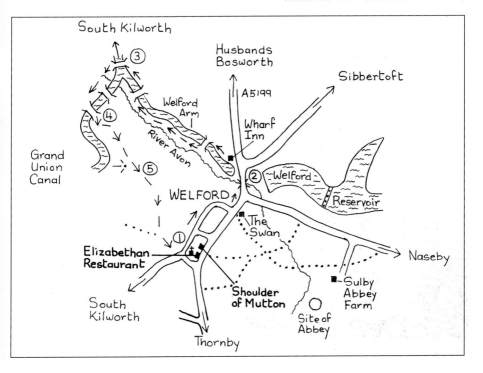

❸ At the junction with the Leicester branch of the Grand Union, cross the bridge to join the towpath and turn left. If you feel like diverting for refreshment, North Kilworth narrow boat base is ½ mile up the canal to the right.

❹ Leave the canal at the second bridge, about ½ mile along. Cross over the bridge and follow the broad track. This first bends left and then follows alongside the hedge, keeping it on the left and then on the right.

❺ After about ¾ mile with wonderful views, the grassy track comes out on a concrete road to a farm on your left. Continue straight ahead downhill towards Welford. Coming into the village, turn left along West End to reach the church.

COTTESBROOKE

Length: 6 miles

Getting there: Cottesbrooke lies 10 miles north of Northampton, just east of the A5199. Turn through Creaton and follow signs to Cottesbrooke.	**Parking:** On quiet roadsides in the village.	**Map:** OS Landranger 141 Kettering and Corby (GR 711735).

Midway between Northampton and Market Harborough, and 10 miles from each, Cottesbrooke seems the heart of rural England. The main road through the village is a gated road to the tiny hamlet of Haselbech – little traffic passes this way. Along the road are blended pretty thatched cottages and old brown sandstone houses and at their centre, a grey medieval church surrounded by dark green yews. Beside the church is the old rectory built around 1740, and of a similar age is the red sandstone Grange opposite. And behind all these stands Cottesbrooke Hall, a beautiful Queen Anne mansion, said to have been the model for Jane Austen's

FOOD and DRINK

The Stag's Head at Maidwell is a pleasant and friendly roadside pub with a large garden. The surprise here is the extensive menu, comprising traditional fare and 'Dishes from around the World'. It's not often you can get chow mein in an English country pub! Several other countries are represented of course, and the food is attractively served – all under the watchful eye of that Stag! Telephone 01604 686219.

Mansfield Park. It was built around 1702 by Sir John Langham, the architect most probably being Francis Smith of Warwick.

At the heart of the village is the church of All Saints dating from 1220. You will need to get a key to see inside, but your effort will be well repaid. Once through the door, you will see 'one of the most complete Georgian interiors in the Midlands'. There are high box pews (the children must have enjoyed being so well concealed during the sermon!), a three-tier pulpit and a squire's pew complete with fire grate. Of course there are many memorials to the Langham family.

The walk starts from the church and passes through the main part of this attractive village. After leaving the parkland of Cottesbrooke Hall, you climb Haselbech Hill, the highest point for miles around. From the top, there are good views of Haselbech Hall to the north, but on the descent into Maidwell, a wonderful panorama opens before you. You may well wish for your binoculars! This is a fine place for a picnic. When at last you reach the bottom of the hill, you return on a well-surfaced bridleway through the valley. Just before reaching the village, there are good views of Cottesbrooke Hall in its grounds.

THE WALK

❶ With the church on your left, walk downhill and through the main part of the village. Keep straight on, ignoring roads to the left, and cross Cottesbrooke Park land on a gated road. Keeping straight ahead, the road climbs Haselbech Hill.

❷ Just over the summit of the hill, take the bridleway to Maidwell on the right. This is at first a gravelled track to various houses. Disregard all tracks on the right, and eventually you reach the last house, which is a white bungalow. Looking left from this point onwards will give you fine views of Haselbech Hall.

❸ Here the bridleway branches right to cross a field. You should not miss it – there are no fewer than five waymarks on the gate. Through the field gate on the opposite side, the grassy bridleway ahead is obvious. Follow it along the field edges to a junction of bridleways.

❹ Take the bridleway on the left, signposted to Maidwell. As you descend the hill, there are magnificent views with the spire of Saxon Brixworth church away

PLACES of INTEREST

Cottesbrooke Hall – or at least its gardens – should not be missed if you are visiting the village. The Hall is renowned for its fine collection of sporting paintings (Ben Marshall and Stubbs in particular), 18th-century English and French furniture and fine porcelain. The excellence of the gardens matches that of the Hall. Exotic plants are for sale and tea is served in the Old Laundry. Hall and gardens are open on Thursday afternoons, the gardens alone at other times also. Telephone 01604 505808.

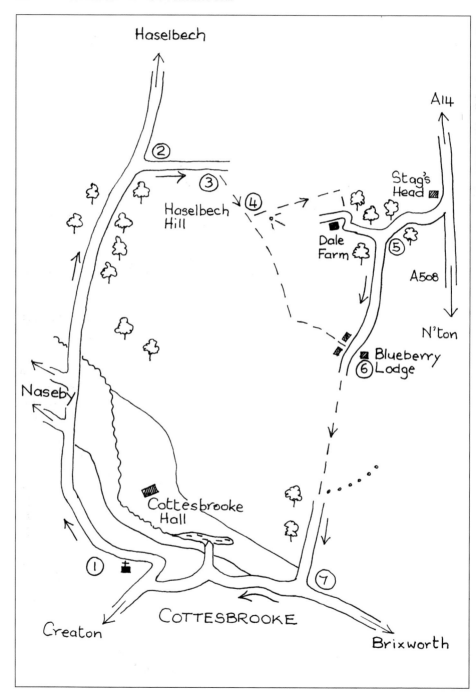

Cottesbrooke Hall.

on the horizon. The bridleway clearly follows the field edges and is well-directed around the back of a farm. Past the farm, continue downhill along the field edge. At the bottom, a plethora of signs encourages you to turn left. Do not do so! Continue ahead and the track soon swings right to come out near the brick buildings of Dale Farm. Cross the front of the farm on the tarmacked road and turn downhill.

❺ At the junction in the woodland at the bottom of the hill there are two choices. If you wish to visit the Stag's Head at Maidwell, continue straight ahead for ½ mile. To continue with the walk, turn right and follow the tarmacked road to Blueberry Lodge. There should be little traffic – the road serves only the Lodge.

❻ At Blueberry Lodge, continue on the grassy bridleway. This crosses fields and then reaches a wood, after which the track surface becomes gravelled and then tarmacked. Continue straight ahead to the road.

❼ At the road, turn right and soon you will have a splendid view of Cottesbrooke Hall on the right. Shortly you will pass the entrace to the Hall. At the end of the 19th century the Hall was let for some time – for a few years to the famed Elisabeth, Empress of Austria, who took it as her 'hunting box', Cottesbrooke being the centre of the famous Pytchley Hunt. Not only hunting but racing was an important pastime around Cottesbrooke, and it is said that here a local race was the forerunner of the Grand National. The Hall is presently owned by the Macdonald-Buchanan family, who bought it in 1937. Both Hall and gardens certainly merit a visit if they are open, but if not, you can just glimpse the lake and ornamental bridge from the gates.

When you come to the road junction in the village, turn right to return to the church.

THE BRAMPTONS

Length: 3½ miles

Getting there: Chapel Brampton lies on the A50, 4 miles north-west of Northampton.

Parking: The roads in the villages are quite busy, although it may be possible to park along the main Welford Road. There is good parking at the railway station on the Pitsford Road, which is the start of the walk, east of the A50.

Map: OS Landranger 152 Northampton and Milton Keynes (GR 730663 Chapel Brampton).

On a low hill just to the north-west of Northampton are found the twin villages of Church and Chapel Brampton. The roads are lined with houses of warm Northampton sandstone and those fortunate enough to live there are provided with two golf courses and a riding stables

for their recreation. Dormitory villages, you might think, and for a desirable place to live within easy reach of Northampton you need look no farther. But we should look farther, a lot farther back into time.

The Romans, too, liked the Bramptons. Aerial photographs show more

---

FOOD and DRINK

The Spencer Arms at Chapel Brampton is oozing with atmosphere in the form of low beams, candlelight and Spencer paraphernalia. It is a large and very popular establishment with a suitably extensive menu served at all times. Here you may be tempted to Mediterranean swordfish steaks or vegetarian green Thai curry. There are many other 'snacks' (try the Italian open sandwiches!) and even cream teas are served. Telephone: 01604 846759).

Down at the railway station, the Brampton Halt is now a pub serving meals. The menu is not wide, but it is interesting, and the atmosphere of an old railway station is, to say the least, different. There is also lots of space for outside dining here. Also at the railway station, the Platform Three Buffet offers drinks and light refreshments on days when the railway is operational.

The Village Stores on Back Lane in Chapel Brampton will provide you with at least enough for a reasonable picnic.

---

cropmarks, indicative of Roman and pre-historic occupation, around the Bramptons than in any other part of Northamptonshire. There have, of course, been numerous 'finds' in the villages.

Prosperity was brought to the Bramptons at the end of the 18th century when the London-Ireland mail coaches began to pass this way. They might have been expected to go via the old Roman road, Watling Street, but this was in a poor state of repair at this time. Within a few years, there were several coaches a day. Chapel Brampton became a staging post, and the Old Posting House can still be seen on the Welford Road. It offered stabling and accommodation, food and drink for the passengers. We can picture the stage coaches arriving. They clattered up the hill from the river bridge and sounded the post horns to summon attention as they entered the village. There would be passengers both inside and on top, and they would be tired and probably dusty or muddy. The activities at the Posting House must have provided employment and much excitement for the villagers.

There were few houses in the villages before this time. Most of them belonged to the Spencer estates at nearby Althorp. The Spencer Arms was a rough village inn and ale-house called the Stag's Head – a far cry from today!

Both villages have a wealth of interesting buildings. At Church Brampton the church itself is 14th-century and dedicated to St Botolph, the saint of travellers – a dedication largely found in East Anglia. There is much to see inside, and a welcome leaflet to guide you around it all.

This walk takes you through both villages, past the church and most of the interesting buildings. Starting from the old railway station on the Pitsford Road, you walk along the Brampton Valley Way. The route then leads across fields and up a track to Brampton Hill, from which there are good views all around. You then descend into Church Brampton past the site of an old Roman villa and continue through that village and back along a bridleway to Chapel Brampton.

THE WALK

❶ From the station, cross the railway line and turn left. This is the Brampton Valley Way, along the line of the old Northampton to Market Harborough railway. At Merry Tom Crossing, leave the Brampton Valley Way and take the lane to the left. After 300 yards, follow the

The start of the walk.

footpath signed on the left, uphill and over three fields to the road. Should the fields be recently ploughed and the path unclear, aim well to the left of the barn at the corner of the fields and maintain this direction.

❷ Cross the road, and turning left, take the lane to Brampton Hill 50 yards along. Where the bridleway crosses this lane, go right. At the track junction, turn left and pass in front of Hill Farm, still following the bridleway.

❸ Follow the obvious track downhill beside the hedges to reach the road. The Roman villa site is on your right. At the road, turn left, and then right down Church Lane to reach the main road. Turn left and follow the road past the church and through the village to a bridleway on the left after the crossroads.

❹ Follow the bridleway along the hedge and across a field to Chapel Brampton. When you reach the road, the drive of the Old Posting House is ahead of you, now with new houses where once there were stables.

❺ At the road, turn left, and then immediately right along Welford Road. The Old Posting House is on your right with the 'Spencer 10' opposite before Cedar Hythe. The 'Spencer 10' (really 20, as there is another set in Church Brampton) are houses built by the 4th Earl Spencer in the mid-1800s for his employees. This was a most generous provision as each one had its own shed and pigsty! In No 1 lived the school teacher –

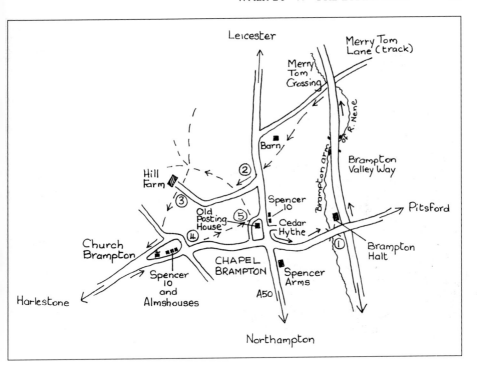

the old school stood beside it, near the entrance to Cedar Hythe now. Cedar Hythe itself is of interest. It was built in 1967 on the site of the former Brampton Hall and later Brampton House – the old surrounding wall can still be seen on the Pitsford Road. The new estate itself won a National Award for Architecture. There is also some evidence that St Margaret's chapel, the 'chapel' of Chapel Brampton, stood on this site. Pass them all and turn left down Pitsford Road to return to the station.

PLACES of INTEREST

The **Northampton and Lamport Railway** runs steam and diesel locomotives on Sundays from the Pitsford and Brampton station on the Pitsford Road, where the walk starts. The track runs alongside the Brampton Valley Way and journey time is about 20 minutes. Perhaps a bonus for the end of the walk. Telephone 01604 820327.

Two miles west, on the road to East Haddon, is **Holdenby House and Gardens**. Built by Sir Christopher Hatton to entertain Elizabeth I, it was once the largest house in England. The house is fascinating, the gardens are beautiful, and there is also a falconry centre, a 17th-century farmstead (complete with smells!), a working armoury, other craft workshops, a museum, a miniature train and much more. Telephone: 01604 770074.